# THE SIKHS

# THE SIKHS

BY

GENERAL

**SIR JOHN J. H. GORDON, K.C.B.**

*WITH ILLUSTRATIONS BY THE AUTHOR*

GYAN

*Published by*

Gyan Publishing House
5, Ansari Road
Daryaganj, New Delhi-110002
Phone: 011-47034999, 9811692060
E-mail: books@gyanbooks.com

*Distribution Network*
gyanbooks.com
India, USA, Canada, UK, Australia



ISBN: 978-81-212-4920-1 (HB)
First Published, 1904

2nd Impression 2024

*Printed at:* Gyan Press, Delhi.



**THE SIKHS**
Author: JOHN J. H. GORDON

# THE SIKHS

THE NATIONAL HERO OF THE SIKHS—
RANJIT SINGH, MAHARAJA OF THE PUNJAB, 1801-1839.

*After a sketch by the Hon. E. Eden, taken at Lahore, December 1838, during Lord Auckland's visit.*

# THE SIKHS

BY

GENERAL

SIR JOHN J. H. GORDON, K.C.B.

*WITH ILLUSTRATIONS BY THE AUTHOR*

WILLIAM BLACKWOOD AND SONS

EDINBURGH AND LONDON

MCMIV

# PREFACE.

No visitors at the celebration of the King's Coronation in London received a heartier welcome than the soldiers of the many races and classes who so well represented the Indian Army. Our home people were able to see the quality of the men who compose it, while they themselves were enabled to form a clearer conception of Britain's strength and resources and the character of her people. They were supremely pleased at being present on such an auspicious occasion as the crowning of their King-Emperor, and carried away with them, and left behind them, feelings that should draw closer the ties which bind

India and its people to the British Crown. Politically it was a practical gain for all.

Conspicuous among them were the Sikhs, —tall, bearded, dignified-looking men, intelligent and keen observers, — whose soldierly bearing was the admiration of all who beheld them. The name Sikh is reminiscent of very hard fighting against us fifty years ago, and of equally hard fighting for us on many a field since. Belonging to an exceptional as well as a fine martial race, more than ordinary interest is attached to them on account of their origin and religion. In the following pages I have given a short sketch of this warlike race, and of their rise through much tribulation to power as a nation, and transformation by the fortune of war into loyal and hearty subjects of the Great Queen Victoria. In addition to personal notes made during many years' service with Sikhs, I have drawn information from various old works relating to them by Malcolm, Cunningham, M'Gregor, Smyth, and others, and also from the History of the Punjab by Syad Muhammad Latif and Dr Trumpp's Translation of the 'Granth,' the Sacred Book of the Sikhs.

J. J. H. GORDON.

35 Onslow Square, London,
1*st September* 1904.

# CONTENTS.

# ILLUSTRATIONS.

# THE SIKHS.

## CHAPTER I.

### ORIGIN OF THE SIKHS.

Of all the many peoples of India none possesses for us greater or more varied historical interest than the Sikhs, a people who four hundred years ago as a reformed religious sect sprang from the ranks of the Jats, a numerous as well as the most important agricultural tribe in the Punjab, descended from the ancient Scythian Getæ. They stand out prominently as men of action, who have preserved inherited racial characteristics foreign to Orientals, and evolved themselves by the strength of their own arms into one of the finest military types to be found anywhere. Their story furnishes a stirring and romantic chapter in the world's history, carrying the imagination back in full flight over the lapse of centuries.

Taking their rise among the disciples of the peaceful Nanak, a Jat Hindu religious reformer, they ultimately, under the pressure of persecution, became a community of warriors, who by the genius of a young Sikh chief, Ranjit Singh, were welded into a nation at the dawn of the nineteenth century. After they lost his strong guiding hand they struggled desperately with us for supremacy in several pitched battles on the Sutlej in 1845-46, when we found them indeed foemen worthy of our steel. Though then disastrously defeated, they doggedly clung to the idea that, after all, they were a match for the British, and rose a second time three years later. Again they fought with all their vigorous might, but being completely vanquished in the open field, they then, like brave men as they are, submitted to the decree of war, and in 1849 were absorbed with the Punjab into the British Indian Empire. They rose a third time in 1857, but then it was shoulder to shoulder with us to aid in beating down the revolt of our native army in Hindostan, when they flocked in thousands to the standards of their late conquerors at the summons of Sir John Lawrence, the great Pro-Consul of the Punjab, whose good government had converted them in a few years into loyal subjects of the British Crown. None have fought more stoutly and stubbornly against us, none more loyally and gallantly for us, than the Sikhs. They have taken part with us in many a "far-flung battle-line" in Asia and Africa, and become the symbol to India of all that is loyal and courageous. Wherever there has been hard fighting to be done, there they have been found in the forefront, maintaining their high reputation for steadfast fidelity, dogged tenacity, and dauntless courage,—the undying heritage of the Sikhs. As they fought for their Gurus and for their

Maharaja, so they have fought for Britain. Loyalty is in their blood.

The Punjab—the land of the five rivers, as the name signifies—is the home-land of the Sikhs. Through it passes the great highway from Central Asia, along which from the remotest antiquity invading hosts have marched bent on the plunder and conquest of India. In prehistoric times hordes of Aryans and Scythians surged through its northern mountain gateways. There Alexander and his Greeks fought and conquered, annexing it as a province of Macedon, while from the eleventh to the eighteenth century Afghan, Tartar, and Persian armies made it the scene of incessant war. There the battles were fought for the rich prize of Hindostan. Bred in a locality which has had to bear the brunt of every invasion, and imbued with the traditions of these long centuries of tumult, the peasantry were as proficient with the sword as with the plough, passing to and from the pursuits of war and peace according to the times.

The origin of the Jat tribe has been the subject of much discussion among distinguished oriental writers, but the weight of authority is all in favour of it being a relic of the Scythians, who at various times before and after the Christian era, swarming off from their camping-grounds in High Asia, pushed their way into the Punjab and established their dynasties there with the northern form of Budhism. The Indo-Aryans, who had occupied India many centuries before, vainly attempted to stem the torrent of these fresh invaders from the north, and waged constant war with them until, according to ancient legendary history, they gained a great victory in the middle of the sixth century A.D. and "freed India from the Huns," by which name these Scythians were also known. After this Budhism gradually gave way to the ascendancy of the Brahmans, under whose influence Hinduism had lost all resemblance to the simple old religion taught in the Vedas—the worship of one Supreme and only God.

We have but a dim outline of these early times from ancient Indian literature, Greek and Chinese writers, traditions, temple inscriptions, and coins. A portion of the Scythian invaders, descendants of the Massa-Getæ of old Asia, were called Getes, from whom the modern Jats are said to have sprung, the name having been so transposed in progress of time. Arrian, the Greek historian of Alexander's campaign in Asia, mentions that the Getes, the Indo-Scythes as he terms them, who served as allies of Darius, formed the *élite* of his army in the great battle of Arbela on the Tigris, 331 B.C., when the Persian Empire, which then extended into the Punjab, was overthrown by Alexander. He dwells with pleasure on Indo-Scythic valour. Colonel Tod, the most scholarly of Indian writers on the old races, in his classical 'Annals of Rajasthan,' compiled eighty years ago, identifies the Jats of his day with the ancient Scythian Getæ of Central Asia mentioned by Arrian, tracing their descendants under the names of Gete, Yothi, Yuti, Jote, to Jit and Jat, the last two being those by which the tribe was then known in Rajputana and the Punjab. He also describes an existing old temple inscription which shows that the Jits were in power in the Punjab in the fifth century A.D.,—the memorial of a Jit prince of Lalpura dated 409,—and observes, "These Jit princes of Lalpura in the Punjab were the leaders of that very colony of the Yuti from the Jaxartes who, as recorded by De Guignes, crossed the Indus in the fifth century and possessed themselves of the Punjab." Apparently these Jits were one of the most important of the Scythic tribes, and entered the Punjab in large numbers at the same time as their congeners the Goths were invading Italy. This was their last irruption in force into India. Small bodies of emigrants are said to have continued to follow up to the eleventh century, when the Getic Empire on the Oxus was overwhelmed in the tide of Islamism, many fugitives then fleeing to join their kind in the Indus valley, where they formed a powerful community, as is shown in the interesting records of the first invasion of India by Mahmud of Ghuzni, in the eleventh century, which led to the occupation of Lahore, and the establishment of the Mahomedan Empire in India after a struggle on the frontier lasting for two centuries.

The Jats now emerged from the nebulous region of their history, and henceforward they were never lost to sight. At every step taken by the Mahomedan invaders from the north they encountered the Jats, who showed themselves a power to be reckoned with. They so vigorously opposed Mahmud's army in the passage of the Indus, and harassed his line of march, that he had in person to lead his troops against them in 1027. The famous Tamerlane in the fourteenth century, at the head of his mighty Tartar host, felt their weight, and waged a war of extermination against them; while the Emperor Baber in his Memoirs writes in 1525 that in all his expeditions into India he was assailed by multitudes of Jits. These Afghan and Moghul invaders knew them by the name of Jits, but they were then known in the Punjab as Jats. Their early settlements were along the whole valley of the Indus from the north down to Sindh. Pliny and Ptolemy in their writings mention the Jatii of these regions. By the sixteenth century they had spread over the Punjab to the deserts of Rajputana and south to the banks of the Jumna as the results of wars and tumults following the Moslem invasions, when they were brushed aside for the time. To-day they are found in all these localities rooted to the soil. Among them the tradition is still strong of the Central Asian region being the cradle of their race. As the latest comers from the bracing north, recruited for several centuries by fresh blood, and established in a climate less liable to lead to deterioration than that of the plains of Hindostan, the Jats have maintained their hardy northern strain, and with it physical superiority and force of character.

The Indo-Aryans, who had settled in India many centuries earlier, about 1500 B.C., looked on these Scythian invaders with scorn as inferiors, and termed them "excluded heretics." In the estimation of the orthodox Hindus the Jats hold an inferior social position below that of their leading castes. Their customs, habits, and indulgences, prohibited by the ordinances which govern the ordinary Hindus, go to confirm the tradition of their Getic origin; for though there may be nothing of the Scythian in their language, there is undoubtedly much in their customs, which have survived long after the old tongue has disappeared through changes in dynasties and religion. There is, therefore, the strongest ground for assuming that this warlike Jat tribe of to-day, to which the Sikhs belong, are the descendants of the Getæ, the most conspicuous of the races of ancient Asia, whose bravery in fighting the Greeks hand to hand elicited the warm admiration of the Macedonian generals, as related by Arrian. Wars and anarchy failed to destroy them. They have braved the storms of centuries and preserved continuity with the past, emerging at last from barbarism into light, civilisation, and good government under the British Crown as an industrious, bold, and loyal people who have never broken with their traditions for tenacious energy and military virtues, and who to-day furnish us with thousands of splendid soldiers fit to go anywhere and stand in line against any enemy.

The rise and progress of the Sikhs present one of those strange repetitions which have occurred in the life of nations; for though in a precise sense they were at first but a religious sect, later on, bound together by the additional tie of military and political organisation, they, as a united people, recruited from the most important race in the Punjab, were, under the master hand of their Maharaja, Ranjit Singh, converted into an individual nation when the decay of the Moghul Empire gave this Jat Sikh chief the opportunity to establish a territorial dominion over the regions colonised and ruled in former times by his ancestors, the ancient Jits.

## CHAPTER II.

### NANAK THE REFORMER, FOUNDER OF THE SIKH SECT.

The Sikh religion originated with the teaching of Nanak, who from being a wandering Hindu devotee settled down about the year 1500 as a missionary preacher to his countrymen, proclaiming a deistic doctrine, embracing what was best in the two ancient faiths of Hindu and Budhist — the personal God of the one and the spiritual equality of the other. He was born in 1469 in a village near Lahore in the Punjab, the son of a Jat farmer and small trader. As a boy he was thoughtful, reserved, and inclined to devotion. He early showed the bent of his mind by puzzling his teacher with questions as to the existence of God. At the age of nine he shocked the family Brahman priest by refusing to be invested with the sacred thread at the Hindu ceremony of initiation, contending that it was a useless form. As a youth, to the distress of his father, he was antagonistic to the ways of the world, despising money-making. Later on marriage failed to divert his mind from the religious turn. He then at the age of thirty-two became a public preacher, and, garbed as a fakir, left his home to attain religious wisdom by travel and intercourse with others in foreign lands, accompanied by four companions as disciples, one of them being the family bard. His sayings and the verses he composed in praise of God were sung by this minstrel to the sound of the *rabab,* or Eastern lute, as he said the "skill of the strings" was necessary to attract listeners. His family now looked on him as mad. In his ardent desire to find a resting-place among the conflicting creeds of men he wandered over all India, and visited Ceylon, Mecca, Persia, and Kabul. The story is told of him that while at Mecca the Kazi observed him asleep with his feet towards the holy Kaaba, the object of Mahomedan devotion. He was angrily roused, abused as an infidel, and asked how he dared to dishonour God's house by turning his feet towards it. "Turn then, if you can, in a direction where God's house is not," was his reply.

On returning to his home after his wanderings he threw aside the garb and habits of the fakir, saying that the numerous religions and castes which he had seen in the world were the devices of men; that he had read Mahomedan Korans and Hindu Purans, but God was nowhere found in them. All was error. He now taught his followers that abandonment of the world after the manner of ascetics was quite unnecessary; that true religion was interwoven in the daily affairs and occupations of life; that God treated all men with equal favour; and that between the hermit in his cell and the king in his palace no difference was made in respect of the kingdom to come. "God will not ask man of what caste or race he is. He will ask him what he has done." As a man sows, that shall he reap. He contended against the furious bigotry of the Mahomedans and the deep-rooted superstition and caste thraldom of the Hindus, and aimed at reforming and reconciling the two creeds. He proclaimed the unity of God and the equality of all men before God; condemned idolatry and inculcated a righteous religious life with brotherly love to one another. He said he was but a man among men, mortal and sinful as they were; that God was all in all, and that belief in the Creator, self-existent, omnipresent and omnipotent, without beginning and everlasting, was the only way to salvation—the one thing needful being firm reliance on God, who was to be worshipped in spirit and in truth; to have abiding companionship with Him, to let His name be continually in their hearts and on their lips, and to pray without ceasing. "The just shall live by faith." This was the keystone of his doctrine.

He now no longer avoided society, but lived as the head of his family and as a patriarch, preaching openly at all the country fairs in his neighbourhood. He met with violent opposition from the Hindu zealots, who reproached him for laying aside the habits of a fakir. "A holy teacher has no defence but the purity of his doctrine. The world may change, but the Creator is unchangeable," was his reply. No Brahman of any note now acknowledged him. The Jat peasantry formed the mass of his disciples. They resorted from all parts, attracted by his preaching, and he soon exercised great influence over vast numbers, who looked on him as their "Guru" or spiritual guide. With their offerings he established almshouses where crowds of the poor and helpless were fed.

He died at his home in 1538, at the age of seventy-one.

He was a contemporary of Luther, and, like the German Reformer, he preached no new faith, but contended that religion had become obscured and transformed during the course of centuries. One of the stories told of him in his crusade against the superstitious ceremonies and forms of the priesthood is that on one occasion seeing some Brahmans at their morning devotions by a stream baling out water with their hands facing the east, going through the ceremony of quenching the thirst of dead clients in another world, he, on the opposite bank, began to do the same facing the west. The Brahmans, thinking him a fakir out of his senses, remonstrated with him, saying that all his labours were in vain, and that he could not hope to relieve the thirst of the departed by such heretical actions. Nanak replied, "I am not giving water to my dead, but irrigating my fields in Kartarpur to prevent them drying up by the scorching heat of the sun." "Watering your fields in Kartarpur, such a long way off! How can these handfuls of water benefit your fields at such a distance?" the Brahmans scoffingly replied. "How can, then, your waters," rejoined Nanak, "reach the next world and quench the thirst of your dead? If the water cannot benefit my crops, which are in this world, how can it benefit your dead in another?"

Nanak's followers were called Sikhs, from *sicsha*, a Sanscrit word signifying disciple or devoted follower, corrupted into Sikh, pronounced Sick, and he was called by them Baba Nanak or Guru Nanak—Father Nanak or the Spiritual guide. When he felt that his end was approaching he appointed as his successor in the Guruship one of his most faithful followers, passing over his two sons despite their remonstrances, one of them being an ascetic and the other a man of the world. He selected whom he thought most fit by moral courage and devotion to the cause to carry on his ministry unimpaired. He did not consider the office he had created a hereditary one, but this was later on brought about by a father's strong affection for a devoted and ambitious daughter. The religion which Nanak founded would have sunk into oblivion, as befell that of other reformers in India before him, but his foresight in creating an apostleship and selecting a successor before his death saved it.

Sikhism had its root solely in religious aspirations. It was a revolt against the tyranny of Brahmanism. On throwing off the yoke, Nanak and his disciples reverted instinctively to the old theistic creed of their ancestors. The simple-minded Jat peasantry to whom he spoke were inclined to the reception of religious reform. Brahmanism was not so deep-rooted in them as in the mass of Hindus in Hindostan; regard for caste was weak, that of tribe and race strong. Their old Getic faith had left a lasting impression on their independent character which profoundly modified their beliefs as Hindus, for the ancient Getes, according to Herodotus, were Theists, and held the tenets of the soul's immortality. With the spread and ascendancy of Hinduism idolatry and priestcraft reigned supreme, and caste exclusiveness, with its narrow restrictions, pressed heavily on the lower classes, who had little consolation to hope for in the next world for the hardships of the present.

As the period between the downfall of Budhism and the advent of Islam was of comparatively short duration, the doctrine of the innate superiority of Brahmanism was rudely shaken by the success of the Mahomedan invaders, inspired with the religious zeal of their new faith, proclaiming the unity of God, denouncing idolatry, and disregarding the bonds of caste. Early in the fifteenth century Hindu reformers had risen in Hindostan who seized upon the doctrine of man's equality before God, assailed the worship of idols, the authority of Hindu Shasters and Mahomedan Koran, and the exclusive use of a learned language in religious books unintelligible to the lower orders. They strove to emancipate men's minds from priestcraft and polytheism, and advanced in some measure the cause of enlightenment. The people were appealed to in their own tongue and told that perfect devotion was compatible with the ordinary duties of the world. These reformers passed away and left no successors, but their writings were very popular among the people from being in a spoken language. Nanak's susceptible mind had been influenced by these writings, some of which were afterwards embodied in the sacred book of the Sikhs.

Nanak was the only Hindu reformer who established a national faith. He rose out of the dust as a great preacher with a great theme which he boldly proclaimed, waking up the people to a higher notion of religion. It is a strange coincidence that from being a Hindu devotee he did so at the very time when Luther, the

German monk, nailed his famous theses to his church door at Wittenberg, starting the Reformation in the West, both intent on denouncing what they considered the errors in their religions. His preaching attracted the attention of the Mahomedan governors, who reported that a fakir preaching doctrines at variance with Hindu Vedas and Mahomedan Koran was gaining much influence among the peasantry, which might prove serious to the Government. At that time Baber with his conquering Moghuls was entering the Punjab from the north. He was summoned to Delhi to appear before the Emperor, who after hearing him ordered him to be confined in prison. There he remained for seven months, until Baber captured Delhi and established the Moghul power. Baber interviewed him, when he defended his doctrine with firmness and eloquence. He was released, returned to his home, and continued his ministry.

He extricated his disciples from the accumulated errors of ages. Regarding them merely as disciples, he had no views of political advancement. As a preacher of peace and goodwill to man he told them to "fight with valour, but with no weapon except the Word of God," an injunction to which his successors in the apostleship later on, when driven by persecution to defend themselves, added, "and with the sword of the Lord." His care was to prevent his people from contracting into a sect or into monastic distinctions, proving this by excluding his son, a meditative ascetic, from the ministry after him—the son who justified his fears by becoming the founder of a sect called "Oodasses, indifferent to the world," still existing in considerable numbers, proud of their origin, and using the 'Granth,' but not regarded as genuine Sikhs.

Nanak's line of the Bedi clan through his younger son has been preserved to the present day. During these four hundred years they have been held in much venera-

BABA SIR KHEM SINGH, BEDI, K.C.I.E.,

LINEAL DESCENDANT IN THE FOURTEENTH GENERATION FROM BABA NANAK, THE SIKH REFORMER.

tion by all Sikhs, trusted and protected in the stormy times out of regard for their ancestor. An interesting personality at the recent Coronation celebration in London was Baba Sir Khem Singh, Bedi, K.C.I.E., one of the representatives sent from the Punjab, an old man of great influence and of proved loyalty, who has stood by the British Government from the day, as he expressed it, since the line of Ranjit Singh was ended —the lineal descendant in the fourteenth generation from the Sikh reformer, and the present head of the family. He spoke with decision for his co-religionists, of their fervid loyalty and of their readiness to prove it again and again in the future as they had done in the past, in defence of the King-Emperor and his kingdom. Recently in the columns of a Punjab newspaper he has expressed his conviction that the political object which led the Sikhs to adopt a military life—viz., the establishment of a perfectly peaceful Government and the maintenance of a rule of justice and religious toleration—has been completely realised under the benign reign of the British Government, and that the Sikhs, fully regarding that Government as a god-send, have accordingly placed themselves entirely at its service.

# CHAPTER III.

## SPREAD OF SIKHISM.

NINE Gurus, all Jats, followed Nanak in succession during a period of 170 years, the tenth and last being the martial Govind Singh, who, after creating the religious military commonwealth of warrior Singhs, declared the dispensation ended. He instituted the distinction between a Sikh and a Singh, for every Sikh is not a Singh. All profess the religion of Nanak, but the Singh in addition has by baptism become a Govindhi Sikh, a Singh of the Guru, a lion of his race.

Nanak's successor as Guru was a humble labouring man, who spread the religion by scrupulously adhering to his master's doctrine and commands. Before his death he, also deeming neither of his sons worthy of the office, nominated as successor one of his most earnest followers, a petty carrier by trade,- who sent out many chosen disciples as missionaries to sow the seed of the Sikh faith. His daughter, to whom he was devotedly attached, married Ram Das, a Jat youth of good family of the Sodhi sept of the tribe, who became a zealous Sikh. The Guru at her request not only nominated him his successor, but also made the office hereditary in her offspring. Under Ram Das, who became the fourth Guru in 1574, the Sikhs greatly increased, and by their offerings he was enabled to live in state. He was of a quiet and peaceful disposition, given to literary pursuits, and devoted to the interests of the community. He laid the foundation of the city of Amritsar (Nectar Tank) upon a site granted to him by the tolerant Emperor Akbar, and excavated the holy tank, from which the town derives its name. In its midst on a small island he erected a temple, the future centre of Sikh devotion. He died in 1581, after having appointed his son Arjun as his successor. The Guruship had now become hereditary.

Arjun, the fifth Guru, established himself at Amritsar and completed the sacred tank and temple. A flourishing town grew up around, which became the rallying-point of the Sikhs, who had now rapidly increased in numbers and importance. Up to this time the Gurus led a quiet life, averse to outward show, but Arjun, by means of the wealth resulting from the offerings of increased numbers of disciples, lived as a prince, and kept a numerous band of adherents about him. He was now looked upon by them as a king as well as spiritual leader. With system and method he organised them into a community, and in order to raise their status, to separate them from the mass of Hindus, and to unite them by one common religious tie, he compiled a sacred code written in the mother tongue of the Jats. In this was incorporated the sayings and Psalms of Nanak, his own compositions, and those of the other Gurus, with selected literary productions of the religious reformers of the age whose memory was still fresh in the minds of the people. This supplanted the Hindu Vedas and Puranas which the unlettered people were unable to read. He named it the 'Granth,' the Holy Book, which to the present day is held in the greatest veneration by the Sikhs as binding on all true disciples. He also instituted daily public worship at the temple of the sacred tank at Amritsar, where crowds came daily to bathe, when the 'Granth' was recited all day long with songs of praise to the accompaniment of stringed musical instruments.

Up to this time the income of the Guru proceeded from voluntary offerings. He now reduced this to a regular religious tax levied by deputies appointed in the various districts, who presented the amount to the Guru in the annual General Assembly at Amritsar. The Sikhs were thus gradually accustomed to a domestic government of their own, and began to feel themselves an organised and strong party. The teaching of the new faith having met with much success and taken firm root among the Jat peasantry by means of this secular policy, the Guru's personal power and means greatly increased, thereby attracting public attention to him. Accordingly he excited the jealousy and enmity of the imperial Governor of Lahore, was charged with treason in espousing the cause of the Emperor's rebel son in one of the numerous family disputes among the Moghuls, and thrown into prison at Lahore, where he died in 1606, his death being ascribed to torture. His last message to his people was, "God is the strength of the strengthless; He neither cometh nor goeth,—He is permanent ever." His death was looked upon as that of a martyr to the faith. It inflamed the religious passions of the peaceful sect, converting them into a warlike community ready to defend their religion with the sword. This became the turning-point of their history, and developed the struggle which changed the whole character of the reformatory movement.

Har Govind succeeded his father as sixth Guru in 1606, and found himself at the head of a powerful and widespread religious order whose influence was felt far and near. Of a warlike spirit, he armed his followers and inspired them with his own spirit of revenge and of hatred to their oppressors. At an audience with the Moghul Emperor he proved the treachery against his father and secured the execution of his powerful murderer. Political leadership now developed in the young Guru, who assumed the character of a soldier, while his Sikhs became a brotherhood in arms as in faith. Like a fighting bishop of the middle ages, he led his warriors in person when impelled to play a part which was probably judged on both sides to be expedient, and took service in the Moghul army. After a time he fell under suspicion, and the Emperor imprisoned him in Gwalior Fort for twelve years. On being released at the accession of a new Emperor he re-entered the Moghul service, but later on, suspecting treachery, he fled to Amritsar, where the Sikh ecclesiastical headquarters had remained under the system established by his father.

On three occasions after desperate fighting he defeated the royal troops sent against him. He was now looked upon as a hero and a master of the art of war, and the Sikhs were always ready to rally round his banner; but being satisfied with his success so far, and knowing the strength and resources of the Government, he retired to the sub-Himalayan hills to preserve his power and recruit his followers. The sect had now risen to the dignity of persecution, and, despite repressive measures, crowds of Jat peasantry joined it.

Har Govind quite changed the character of the peaceful Nanak's disciples, who now laid aside their rosaries and buckled on the sword in defence of their faith. His popularity increased with the warlike Jats, who, oppressed in their villages, joined him in large numbers. The camp became their home and the plunder of the Mahomedans their lawful prey. He died in 1638, after nominating as his successor his grandson, son of his eldest deceased son. The fighting spirit of the Sikhs having been roused and their quality proved, made them a power to be courted. Under their Guru they joined a son of the Emperor in rebellion, who was friendly to them, but eventually had to flee to their retreats. On the death of their leader his young son, six years of age, succeeded him as eighth Guru; but a contest now arose among the Sikhs regarding the succession, which, curiously enough, was referred to the arbitration of the Moghul Emperor, who summoned the boy to Delhi, where he died.

Tegh Bahadur, the younger son of the martial Har Govind, was now selected as ninth Guru. His mother, when the succession went some years before to Har Govind's grandson, remonstrated at the decision; but the dying Guru gave his arms to her to keep for her son Tegh Bahadur, who, he said, would yet become Guru. Tegh Bahadur demurred at first to accept the office, saying that he would rather be Degh Bahadur (Lord of the Cooking-Pot—"Hospitality") than Tegh Bahadur (Lord of the Sword), meaning that he preferred to support the poor and feed the hungry. The assembled Sikhs hailed this as a most auspicious offer of unbounded hospitality, and acted up to their maxim of "Jiska degh us ka tegh" (My sword is at the service of him who feeds me) by flocking in great numbers to his banner. He built a fort near the Sutlej, there established his ecclesiastical and military headquarters, and continued the fitful life of struggle with the hated Mahomedans. He was captured and led to Delhi in 1675, where, on refusing to abjure his religion, he was beheaded by order of the Emperor. Before leaving he sent for his young and only son Govind, then fifteen years of age, and girding on him the sword of his father

Har Govind, who had first used it in defence of the faith, hailed him as the future Guru of the Sikhs, as he said he knew he was going to his death, and exhorted him to recover his dead body. (This was done by some daring men of low caste, who were afterwards, as a reward for their courage, enrolled by Govind as "Singhs" under the name of Muzhabi Sikhs, a charter which gave them higher status as brave fighting men. Several thousands of this class are in the Indian army at the present day.)

The dragon's teeth thus sown at Delhi in the blood of the martyred Guru, Tegh Bahadur, soon brought to harvest an abundant crop.

## CHAPTER IV.

### GURU GOVIND SINGH, FOUNDER OF THE KHALSA, THE SIKH COMMONWEALTH.

YOUNG Govind, who became the tenth Guru on the death of his father, Tegh Bahadur, in 1675, being surrounded by enemies, retired to the Himalayas at the head-waters of the Jumna, and there lived for twenty years, devoting himself to study and the chase. At the age of thirty-five he issued from his retreat, having matured his plans for reforming the Sikhs and making them a separate people. The violent death of his father and the deep sense of the wrongs of his persecuted race resolved him to make them prominent as a nation. He summoned the dispersed Sikhs from all parts to join him: crowds obeyed. The time suited him, the bigot Emperor Aurangzeb having commenced a crusade against Hindu and Sikh alike. He called upon his disciples by all that was dear to them, in defence of their faith and in the name of their martyred Guru to exchange their rosaries and ploughs for swords: now was the time to raise their fallen race and to overthrow the hated Mahomedans, who were bent on subverting their religion. There could be no religious freedom while the Moslem ruled the land.

He then announced that converts to the Sikh faith would be admitted from all tribes, and caste abolished. In order to effect this he revived in the form of baptism an old initiatory ceremony called the *pahal*, which had ceased to be observed during the persecutions, administering it first to five of his most resolute disciples who had given marked proof of devotion. After bathing and putting on clean garments they were seated side by side, each with his sword girded on. With a two-edged dagger the

Guru stirred a mixture of sugar-and-water in an iron dish, reciting over it verses in praise of God.[1] Some of this they drank, part was poured on their heads, and the rest sprinkled on their faces. Then patting them with his hand, he commanded them to say, "The Khalsa of the Vah Guru, victory to the Vah Guru." They were then hailed as "Singhs" or lions of their race, and declared to be the Khalsa—the select, the purified, God's own—the Sikh brotherhood or commonwealth, which he foretold would grow up as a forest of trees firmly rooted, multiplying their leaves, become a nation and rule the land. Govind then took the *pahal* from their hands in the same manner and exclaimed, "The Khalsa arose from the Guru and the Guru from the Khalsa. They are the mutual protectors of each other." All the rest of the

[1] The tradition is that as the water was being poured into the iron dish, Govind's wife happened to pass by carrying five kinds of sugared sweetmeats. She was hailed by him as auspicious. He took some sugar from her hands and mixed it in the baptismal water.

disciples present were similarly baptised and declared Singhs. The Guru then announced that wherever five Sikhs should be assembled together, it should be considered as if the Guru was himself present; that those who wished to see the Guru would see him in the Khalsa. From this time he changed his name to Govind Singh, and he added "Singh" to his baptised followers' names, an affix which up till then was exclusively assumed by the Rajputs, the first military class of the Hindus, who alone were entitled to carry arms.

This baptismal rite is observed to this day—administered when five or more Sikhs are present, and not before the attainment of years of discretion.

The members of the Khalsa were required to carry arms and to salute one another with "The Khalsa is of the Lord Guru, victory attend the Lord!" as an acknowledgment of obligation to the brotherhood. In order to mark them as a select body who should be known by outward signs, it was declared that every true Sikh must always have five things with him, their names all commencing with the letter *k*—namely, *kes* (long hair of the head: the Sikh must never cut his hair or beard); *kangi* (comb), to secure the hair tied up in a knot on the top of the head; *kachh* (breeches reaching to the knee), *kard* (knife), and *kirpan* (sword). Rules of conduct were also enjoined by which they were to be known to all the world. All was designed to give the Sikhs a distinct national character in opposition to the ways of other people, and to keep alive a sense of duty and profession of faith. Hindus and Mahomedans are much given to shaving heads and beards: among the Scythians and ancient Hindus shaving the head was an infamous punishment. "Come out from among them, and be ye separate; take the *pahal* of the Khalsa," was Govind's call to the Sikhs. "I bow with love and devotion to the Holy Sword,"[1] was his

[1] Herodotus refers to the worship of the Sword which prevailed among the Scythian Getæ.

address to the sword, by which religious liberty was to be won; and his prayer enjoined to every Singh, "Grant, O God, that I may never hesitate to perform good and meritorious deeds, nor flee from my enemy in fear when I go to fight with him with the determination and certainty of victory. When the period of life may draw to its close on the field of battle, may I die like a hero. Let us prove our loyalty to our sovereign and master, and leave our life and death to God." His definition of the true Sikh was he who never fears though often overcome. Personal courage in the fight for the cause was to be the highest of virtues, cowardice the basest of crimes. Neither loss of life nor loss of property in maintaining their cause was to be lamented.

Govind's next move was to issue orders that every Sikh house inhabited by four adult males should contribute two for service under him. In a short time 80,000 men were gathered round him. In ad-

GOVIND SINGH'S ARMED DISCIPLES.

THE EARLY SOLDIERS OF THE KHALSA.

dressing them he commenced by praising God as the Omnipotent, Almighty, Invincible, and Merciful, who must be worshipped in truthfulness and sincerity, and that no material resemblance must degrade Him. He could only be beheld by the eye of faith in the general body of the Khalsa. All Sikhs must be united in one chain of brotherhood. "Ye Sikhs are all brothers, all equal; there must be no caste among you, you must all be equal, no man greater than the other. All must eat together and drink from the same cup. Caste must be forgotten, idols destroyed, the Brahmanical thread broken, the graves of saints abandoned, Korans and Purans torn to pieces." The only way to salvation was through the *pahal* [lit. gate] of the true Guru.

He appealed to the eternal human instinct of equality, liberty, and brotherhood, broke for ever with caste prejudices, and received into the Khalsa people of all classes who had hitherto been debarred from bearing arms. The Singhs of the Khalsa felt themselves at once elevated to rank and equality with the proud martial Rajputs. Personal pride and vigour were infused into them, and Sikhism knitted them together in the brotherhood of the Sword. Each became great in his own eyes, as forming one of the select Khalsa whom the Guru regarded as his own. The contagious momentum of enthusiasm created by Govind Singh's irresistible appeal brought thousands of the lower orders to receive the *pahal* and enter the Khalsa. The pride and prejudices of the Brahmans and Rajputs among his followers were offended by this levelling up of caste to such a degree that many of them left him, but he knew that his great strength lay among the Jat peasantry, who welcomed the brotherhood. The disciples who did not acknowledge these innovations of Govind simply called themselves Sikhs, without adding to their names the title of "Singh."

He now disciplined his followers to some

extent, exercised them in the use of arms, organised then into troops and bands, and built forts along the skirt of the hills between the Jumna and the Sutlej where their retreats lay. At the end of the century he felt his power equal to the hazard of a rebellion against the Imperial Government. He routed the hill rajas who opposed him, and defeated the Moghul troops sent to aid them, but the Emperor, roused to greater action, sent a powerful army, which eventually scattered the Sikhs for a time. His mother with his two youngest sons, mere boys, escaped to Sirhind, where they fell into the hands of the Mahomedan governor. One day as they were sitting in his durbar he kindly said to them, "Boys, what would you do if I gave you your liberty?" The boys answered, "We would collect our Sikhs, fight with you, and put you to death." The Governor said, "If you were defeated in the fight, what would you do then?" to which they replied, "We would collect our army again, and either kill you or be killed." The Governor, enraged at this spirited answer, ordered them to be taken away. They were buried alive under a wall, and Govind's mother died of grief.

The Guru himself was hard pressed by the Moghul troops, and held a post with a small devoted band of his men against overwhelming numbers, indignantly refusing to surrender and embrace the Mahomedan faith. His two surviving sons and their mother were killed by his side. Escaping with five followers, he made his way to the jungles and desert south of the Sutlej. He met his adversities with undaunted resolution; submitted to the will of God, and rallied his Sikhs round him again, saying, "The affairs of this sorrowful world are transitory. God makes a thing and unmakes a thing; who are we to grumble since the rein is in His hand? Rely then firmly on His will, for He is the Almighty; what are we poor mortals before Him?" His disciples, seeing their Guru so firm and resolute, recommenced fighting with the enemies of their faith, and defeated the imperial troops sent to disperse them, when great numbers fell on both sides. They were now left there undisturbed for some time, during which thousands of the Jat peasantry joined the Khalsa.

Later on Govind Singh returned to his old retreat near the Sutlej, passing by Sirhind, the scene of the murder of his two little sons. His Sikhs implored him for orders to burn the town. He said that the death of his sons would not be avenged by the destruction of the town, which had done no harm, but that for the future every true Sikh who passed that way should pull down two bricks and throw them into the river in detestation of the crime committed on innocent children. This act has been observed by the faithful Govindi Sikhs through the many years; but little remains now, as the railway contractor some years ago appeared on the scene and carried away the mass of old Sirhind as ballast on which to lay the iron track —the iron made sacred by the martial Guru, and which every true Singh was commanded to wear always in some shape, either as a sword, a small hatchet, or as a bangle. The Sikh now in the railway carriage has the satisfaction of crushing under the wheels the ruins of the cursed city of Sirhind. Towards the close of the reign of his enemy Aurangzeb, Govind Singh remained in peace. He felt it a duty to save all that could be saved of the Sikhs for the time, to recuperate the race, and enable them to emerge more powerful after so much tribulation, as he no doubt saw that the Emperor's bigoted intolerance towards Hindus had weakened the Moghul power. In the meantime he was gaining many disciples, and had given them confidence in fighting. In a letter to the Emperor he wrote, "Beware! I will teach the sparrows to strike the eagle to the ground," an allusion to his inspiring the peasantry with valour and ambition.

Aurangzeb while in the Deccan felt nervous about the Khalsa, and summoned Govind Singh to his Court. He replied in a letter, setting forth the calamities and persecution to which he had been subjected by the Imperial Government. He had been rendered childless and homeless; he had lost all his family. The day of reckoning would at last come when the oppressor would have to account before the Creator for the wrongs done by him; that for himself he despised death and was weary of life; that he feared no one and was willing to die, but that if he was killed his death would be avenged. The Emperor did not resent this letter, but again desired the Guru to come to him, in which case he would be kindly received. He accordingly set out in 1707 to visit Aurangzeb, but on his way he heard of the Emperor's death. The new Emperor, Bahadur Shah, received Govind Singh with distinction, and as he had to contend with the younger brother for the crown, invited his aid and gave him a command of 5000 horse in his army in the Deccan. While there he was mortally wounded by a Pathan assassin. He left no successor; he was the last lineal descendant of the Gurus. He said the appointed ten Gurus of the Sikhs had done their mission, the dispensation was ended, and that he intrusted his beloved Khalsa to the care of God, "the never-dying." "The 'Granth' shall support you in all troubles in this world and be a true guide to the hereafter. The Gurus shall dwell in the society of the Khalsa, and wherever there shall be five Sikhs gathered together there the true Guru shall be present also." They must have "firm belief in one God, and look to the 'Granth' as His inspired law." Feeling faint, he said to his disciples, "Bathe me, put on me new clothes, and arm me with all my weapons. When my breath departs do not take off these clothes, but burn me with them and with all my weapons."[1] He was placed on the funeral

[1] The ancient Scythian custom.

pyre dressed and armed, and expired in the performance of his devotions, his last words being, "O Holy God, Thy mercy is such that though I have not perceived Thee by touch of hand, yet have I fully recognised Thee." He died in 1708 at Nader, on the banks of the Godavari river, in the forty-eighth year of his age, having reigned as Guru for nearly thirty-three years.

The rule of the Gurus had now lasted for two hundred years, and the reformed religion established by them had taken firm root among the Jats. The dry bones of an oppressed peasantry were stirred into life, and the institution of the Sikh baptismal rite at the hands of a few disciples anywhere—in a place of worship, in the house, or by the roadside—brought about the more full and widespread development of the new faith. In Govind were united the qualities of religious leader, king, warrior, and lawgiver. He was the right man for the needs of the Sikhs of his day. He devoted them to steel, and hence the worship of the Sword. He imbued them with a warlike spirit, and made them a people separated from their Indian countrymen in political constitution and ambition as well as in religious tenets, leading them to reject caste and to abandon the institutes of Hinduism for a fraternity of arms and military daring. Faced by the intolerance and persecution of the Moghul Government, the time had gone for the preservation or diffusion of the Sikh faith in Nanak's spirit of meekness and humility. Nanak laid the broad foundations of religious reform, on which Govind built his militant doctrine to suit the changed times. He wished to infuse his own spirit into Nanak's 'Granth,' as he said it only instilled into the minds of the Sikhs a spirit of meekness and humility; but the guardians of the book signed by Arjun the compiler refused to let this be done, so Govind decided to make an additional book for his followers which should rouse their military valour and inflame them to deeds of courage. He completed it in

1696, calling it the 'Granth of the tenth King,' or reign, as the rule of the Gurus is termed — the 'Granth of the Govindi Sikhs,' as distinguished from the 'Adi Granth,' the first book. In it he treats of the knowledge of God and the way to salvation; urges the necessity of leading an active and useful life, giving lofty ideas of social freedom and rousing his disciples to deeds of valour, military glory, and national ascendancy. His 'Book of Guidance' contains the principles by which the Singhs were to adhere to the commands of the Guru in all affairs of life and conduct, and to preserve their separation from all other sects. He instituted the "Guru Mata," or National Council, to which all Sikhs were admitted and given the opportunity to express their opinions on political matters. This with the 'Granth' for guidance formed the Sikh constitution.

By converting a horde of undisciplined peasants into enthusiastic soldiers animated with religious fervour, by inuring them to warfare, and by his new ordinances moulding them into the distinct community of the Khalsa,—the Commonwealth bonded together to fight until they triumphed,—Govind Singh contributed much to the weakening of the Mahomedan power at a time when the Emperor Aurangzeb, by his bigotry towards Hindus, was paving the way for the disintegration of his Empire. Under his strong hand the Sikhs rose by a feeling of nationality among a people who had none. He well and truly laid the corner-stone of that nation which Ranjit Singh a hundred years later, by the force of the religious bond of the Khalsa, raised in the Punjab on the ruins of the Moghul Empire, emancipating the land of his ancestors from thraldom and persecution.

# CHAPTER V.

## STRUGGLES OF THE KHALSA FOR POSSESSION OF THE PUNJAB.

After Govind's death the Khalsa was left without any real head. Such a body with its turbulent elements could not remain quiet, and unfortunately some of them came under the evil influence of a Hindu ascetic, a late Sikh convert and friend of the deceased Guru, who posed as his successor, intrusted by him with the command to avenge his martyred father's blood and that of his young innocent sons. This false apostle appealed to their feelings of revenge, excited at the moment by the circumstances of Govind's death, and led them in a crusade against the hated Mahomedans when the spirit of the ruthless Goth in them flashed out fiercely. They captured Sirhind, the scene of the murder of the Guru's sons, massacred the inhabitants, and then ravaged the country up to Lahore, sparing only those who became Sikhs. The new Emperor, Bahadur Shah, took the field in person against them with a powerful army, called on all Mahomedans to rise in defence of their religion, and gave orders mercilessly to crush the revolt by slaying every Sikh to be found. The death of the Emperor and the usual conflict for the succession among the sons prolonged the anarchy and confusion in the Punjab for six years, during which Mahomedan and Sikh fought with ferocity. At last the Akalis among the Sikhs, a body of fanatical and uncompromising followers of Govind, established by him in the name of his youngest sons, turned against their fiendish leader, alienated by his excesses and attempts to subvert the tenets and commands of their great Guru to suit his Hindu proclivities. His death at the hands of the Moghuls in 1715 ended the struggle. He was an undaunted leader: that is all that can be said in his favour. His memory is not revered by the Sikhs, who looked on him latterly as a heretic. As swords are proved when they bend, so in this case the Sikhs, after having swerved for a time from the path marked out for them by Govind, righted themselves and won in the end.

They now scattered, taking refuge in the hills and jungles, where for about twenty years they remained unorganised, only held together by a common faith and cause, patiently waiting for the opportunity, which came in 1738, when Nadir Shah, the Persian, at the head of his wild host of red-capped warriors, swept through the Punjab to the capture of Delhi. The Sikhs then issued from their retreats and, true to their race traditions, attacked the invaders. On the return march of the conquerors laden with the spoils of the Moghul capital, they fell on the rear of the army and secured much plunder, doubly acceptable to them as being that of accursed Delhi, the scene of the martyrdom of one of their Gurus. "Whence," demanded the imperious Nadir Shah, "come those long-haired barbarians who dare to molest me? Destroy them and their homes." "Their homes are the saddles on their horses' backs," was the reply.

The year 1738 saw the beginning of a new series of Mahomedan invasions from the north. Other invaders followed Nadir up to the close of the century, the Afghans being the last, as seven hundred years before they had been the first under Mahmud of Ghuzni, who introduced his Islamic faith into India. Now commenced the long and fierce contest which was to decide whether the Mahomedan or the Sikh was to rule the Punjab. Much confusion reigned there after the invasion of Nadir. A mortal wound had been inflicted on the Moghul Empire, which was now tottering to its fall. The vigilant Sikhs gathered from all quarters, and again resorted to Amritsar, the cradle of their faith. They formed

KHALSA HORSEMEN MAKING A DASH BY NIGHT TO THE SACRED TANK AT AMRITSAR.

themselves into armed associations and moved about the country, laying towns and villages under contribution. A proclamation was issued by the Lahore Viceroy ordering a general massacre of the long-haired Singhs wherever found. They were hunted like wild beasts, a price being placed on their heads; thousands were put to death, refusing pardon on condition of renouncing their faith and cutting their hair. They were looked on as martyrs to the cause, but, despite all, the Khalsa grew and increased in boldness. Bands of Sikh horsemen were to be seen at dawn riding at full gallop towards Amritsar, running the gantlet of the Mahomedan troops. The message would be sent round the distant villages, "Who will ride to-night?"—the watchword for a dash to be made to bathe in the sacred tank. It is said that no instance was known of a Sikh then captured consenting to abjure his religion. Death was the martyr's crown on such occasions. Henceforth the character of the Sikh resistance completely changed. To defend themselves against the Mahomedan invaders they formed organised confederacies of fighting men, each under one head chief. The necessity of fighting, how to resist, how to practise plunder, was the one law recognised.

In 1748 Ahmad Shah, the Afghan king, aspired to found an Indian Empire, invaded the Punjab, and crossed the Sutlej after capturing Lahore. He was repulsed by the Moghuls and recrossed the Indus. He made two other unsuccessful attempts, and finally in 1756 occupied Delhi, which then suffered a repetition of the former pillage and massacre by the Persians eighteen years before. The Punjab was ceded to the conqueror as the price of peace. This completed the ruin of the Moghul power, which was now reduced to the condition of a province and left a prey to the Mahrattas, who were then overrunning Hindostan. Ahmad Shah returned to Kabul, leaving his son Tymur at Lahore as Viceroy of the Punjab. The confusion and tumult arising from these repeated invasions enabled the Sikh associations to acquire fresh strength by preying on both Moghul and Afghan. No other course was now left to them but to conquer or be conquered. It was war to the knife between them and their new and more robust masters, the Afghans. No quarter was given or asked. Time after time was Amritsar captured, but after each defeat Sikh enthusiasm rose with unabated vigour. When their temple was razed to the ground and the sacred tank filled up with pollution by the blood and entrails of slaughtered cows, they were roused to such a degree that they gathered in thousands, ravaged the country round Lahore, defeated the Afghan troops there, and forced the Viceroy to retreat.

In 1758 the triumphant Sikhs occupied the capital under the leadership of one Jussa Singh, a carpenter, who declared the Khalsa a state. The Moghuls now attempted to recover their lost province, and invited the Mahrattas to aid them in this. They promptly responded with a large force, drove out the Afghans, and occupied the country up to the Indus. All order had now vanished in the Punjab, where Afghans, Moghuls, Mahrattas, and Sikhs were contending for power. The successes of the Mahrattas and Sikhs brought back Ahmad Shah with a numerous army. He drove out the Mahrattas, and following them up, disastrously defeated them at Panipat, near Delhi, in 1761 in one of the most sanguinary battles ever fought in India. He returned to Kabul the same year, leaving a governor shut up in Lahore, the Sikhs having continued active in his rear, swarming round Amritsar and the capital. They now grew more daring, their chiefs appropriating lands and building forts in different parts of the country, which added greatly to their power and resources. Again they restored Amritsar, and assembling there in great force proceeded to attack Sirhind and other places held by the Afghans.

In 1762 Ahmad Shah reappeared, and by rapid marches reached Sirhind, where he routed with great slaughter the Sikh force of 50,000 men besieging that city; then returning by Amritsar, utterly destroyed it. The Sikhs reeled at the blow struck at them, but were strong and confident enough to stand it. Extraordinary vitality was shown by them at this crisis. The prime necessity was to preserve their cause by renewed unremitting effort, and to regain what had been lost. They soon rallied, and once more emerged from the wreckage, beginning life again at Amritsar, and restoring their temple and sacred tank. They then showed what a powerful force character is in the formation of a nation —character moulded by religious persecution and the unflinching courage of the true Sikh, instilled by Govind, "who never fears though oft overcome," which engendered vitality under all conditions, the more adverse the better, with a determination to struggle for the triumph of the Khalsa at all costs.

Thirsting for revenge, they convened a General Assembly and Council, formed a still more compact and formidable confederation, and decided on their plan of campaign. Having assembled a force of 40,000 men, they captured the Pathan strongholds in their neighbourhood, marched to Sirhind, defeated the Afghan troops there, and destroyed that accursed city. They then partitioned out among themselves the country between the Sutlej and the Jumna. This brought back Ahmad Shah with his army; but they retired before him, as they knew they were no match in the open for the better armed Afghans with their artillery.

Sirhind being devastated by Pathan and Sikh alike, the Durrani king now adopted the policy of acknowledging the diplomatic Sikh chief of Patiala as his governor of that province. Disturbances having broken out in Kabul, he, after leaving garrisons in Lahore and Rhotas on the Jhelum, hurriedly departed, the Sikhs as usual harassing his rear. They then captured Lahore, placed three of their chiefs in it as joint governors, and seized all the country between the Sutlej and the Jhelum, exacting fierce retribution from the Mahomedans. A General Assembly was now held at Amritsar, and by a decree the Khalsa was proclaimed the dominant Power in the Punjab and the Sikh religion supreme. This assumption of sovereignty was marked by striking a coin with the inscription, "Guru Govind received from Nanak *degh*, *tegh*, and *futteh* —hospitality, valour, and victory." They had now become masters of the plains from the Jhelum to the Jumna.

In 1767 Ahmad Shah made a final attempt to crush the Sikhs (his eighth invasion), and marching down at the head of his invincible army, engaged them on the banks of the Sutlej and forced them to fall back on their retreats. Failing health now induced him to adopt a policy of conciliation, so he invested the Patiala chief as independent ruler of Sirhind, with the title of Raja of Rajas, with colours and drum, the insignia of royalty, and the right to strike coins; while he confirmed a Sikh chief, who had been one of the joint governors of Lahore, in his possessions in the neighbourhood of that capital, in the vain hope of securing his aid for the Afghan governor he left there. He gave the inch, and the Sikhs soon took the ell: as the powerful Ahmad Shah had commenced to cede, they saw he felt his hold of the Punjab was receding. They cut off the baggage train of his army on its retirement north, and no sooner had he crossed the Indus than they captured Lahore and Rhotas.

Not even the semblance of Afghan dominion now remained in the country between the Indus and the Jumna. The Sikh chiefs spread themselves over it and occupied it as a permanent inheritance, every one of them according to his strength seizing what fell in his way and making himself independent. After a quarter of a century of fierce contest the Sikhs were now relieved from religious persecution. They had survived many a stricken field. Their dogged faith in themselves and in Govind's prophecy that they would become a nation was brought out strongly in the long years of adversity which determined and developed the character of their resistance. The tide had turned at last, and taken at the flood it carried them on to the success which they never doubted would be theirs. They were left undisturbed by their mortal foes the Afghans for the next thirty years, during which time they built up a strong body of clan confederacies, with Amritsar as their central headquarters.

The redoubtable Ahmad Shah of Kabul died in 1773 and was succeeded by his son Tymur, who, deeming it beyond his power to force his way to Lahore, deterred by the wild daring Sikh leaders who had risen, turned his attention to the Lower Punjab, and sent an army of Durranis and Kazalbashes to éxpel the Sikhs from Multan, which they had seized. After repeated attacks he drove them out with severe loss. Shah Zaman, who became King of Kabul in 1793, determined to recover Lahore. After several false starts and some fighting north of the Jhelum he occupied it in 1797, and again in 1798, without opposition; but each time was compelled to return hurriedly to Afghanistan to quell rebellion there. The Sikhs, though powerful for guerilla fighting, were not the equal of the Afghans in training, armament, and disciplined warfare, and retired on the Shah's approach, only to return as he departed and attack and cut off the Afghan posts left behind. During his last invasion he was conciliatory, and his army committed no outrages. Most of the Sikh Sardars accordingly came in and paid homage to him as an honoured guest,—

among them Ranjit Singh, the young chief of a powerful clan, who, by his military ability, address, and tact, attracted the Shah's attention. When his army was returning to Kabul in 1798, for the time unmolested, twelve of his guns stuck in the bed of the Jhelum river. He sent an order to Ranjit Singh to recover them for him, in which case he would consider his wish to be appointed Governor of Lahore. He recovered eight, sent them to Kabul, and as a reward received what he aspired to, a royal investiture as Governor of the capital of the Punjab. The joint Sikh Governors belonging to other clans having reoccupied Lahore on the departure of the Shah, Ranjit Singh in 1799, by combined diplomacy and force, ousted them, and established himself there with his own clan and allies.

# CHAPTER VI.

## THE SIKH CONFEDERACIES—EVOLUTION OF THE SIKH SARDARS.

On the dispersal of the Sikhs a few years after Govind's death they were left without a head to direct them in war. Following on the Persian invasion in 1738, when they again took the field, they organised themselves in bands. Every village produced a sardar or chief with his followers, the boldest and most successful among whom attracted to his banner free-lances from elsewhere to join his party, which gradually grew into a larger one, with greater possessions, by means of raids and plunder under the old simple plan of "let him take who has the power, let him keep who can."

Experience in contending with the in-

A SIKH SARDAR.

vaders taught them the necessity of some measure of union, so these various parties were later on leagued together in twelve confederacies or *misls*, signifying similitude, to imply equality whatever their strength, each being under a chief sardar. Most of these *misls* were called after the villages of their founders, a few being given personal and other names connected with their origin. Every sardar was personally known by the name of his native village. None were admitted as members of these *misls,* which constituted the Khalsa or governing body, unless active horsemen and proficient in arms. After a successful expedition the boldest would ride far and wide to mark the villages they annexed by throwing into them some article to prove the identity of the captor. It was the aim of the daring Jat youths to qualify for admission to a *misl,* and considered by them a religious honour to receive the *pahal* of the Singhs at the hands of a renowned leader. The path to eminence was then open to them.

These sardars did not exercise absolute supremacy over their *misls*, the constitution of which was very democratic and the authority of the chiefs limited. The fighting men exacted a share in the land seized proportionate to the service they had rendered, and merely looked upon the chiefs as leaders in war and arbiters in peace. Many of these chiefs were men of humble birth,—ploughmen, shepherds, or artisans,—all bold stirring men who won their way to be heads of bands of marauding horsemen. They administered according to the law laid down in the 'Granth,' and levied tribute or protection-money from the subdued tracts. All booty taken was divided equally among the chiefs, who in turn subdivided it among their men, who were free to abandon the profession of arms or to transfer their military allegiance from one chief to another,—ever ready to welcome them,—a system of volunteering which was calculated to secure for them good treatment from their chiefs.

The sardars agreed by common consent that some one from among themselves should from time to time be appointed by the popular voice of the Khalsa to the head of Church and State in the National Council at Amritsar, and to be guided by him in all matters requiring united action, thus forming a federal union. The Akalis (Immortals), already referred to, the stern class of zealots which originated as a special body under Guru Govind Singh, formed a National league at Amritsar to maintain the primitive doctrines and reformed worship of the Sikh Church and to watch over the general conduct of the Khalsa. They exercised a fierce scrutiny as censors in upholding strict compliance with the militant creed of the Singhs, constituted themselves defenders of the faith against all innovations, took a prominent part in the Councils, in the planning and arranging of expeditions for averting national danger, and in educating the people in the doctrines of the Sikh religion.

At these Councils business was preceded by the distribution of consecrated bread equally to all present, the "love feast" of the brotherhood, in commemoration of the injunction of Nanak, all bowing the head before the 'Granth,' the Akalis exclaiming, "The Khalsa is of the Lord; victory is of the Lord." When the link of a common enemy was removed the *misls* were often at war among themselves, mutually plundering and disposing of rivals; but notwithstanding the multiplicity of chiefs and their independence, they well understood that union was strength, and that the paramount duty of one and all was to act unitedly in defence of religion and country, being bound by the law laid down in their holy Scriptures to aid one another in the common cause.

All the confederacies had their centres about Lahore, Amritsar, and Sirhind, in the fertile and most populated districts. From there they extended their conquests in every direction, the outlying possessions being

AN AKALI SIKH.

held by minor chiefs. Their strength lay in mobility, most of the Sikhs being good horsemen, armed with sword, spear, matchlocks, and bows. The footmen were employed in holding forts and in following up the cavalry to bring away plunder. The Akalis, always dressed in the sacred blue garments, were heavily armed, and in addition carried several thin sharp-edged quoits (the ancient *discus*) round their turbans, with which they cut down an enemy at a short distance. They kept up the fighting spirit when affairs were not going well, and were the forlorn-hope in many a fight. Some of the *misls* had a few guns taken from the *débris* of retiring armies, but beyond the prestige attached to their possession they were not used in the field. From all accounts these *misldars* were hard drinkers in their times of ease. Tobacco and snuff being Mahomedan indulgences, were expressly forbidden by Govind to his Sikhs, but as a set-off in the way of stimulants they were allowed to drink spirits, prohibited to Moslem and Brahman by their religion, and for this the authority of Nanak was quoted:—

> "Eat and give others to eat,
> Drink and give others to drink,
> Be happy and make others happy."

These drinking-bouts are another relic of their Scythic origin.

Now that the Sikhs were the masters, they treated the Mahomedans with scant consideration, in revenge for former persecution at their hands. They were little better than serfs, only employed as menials, or at best as tenants, to till the ground they had owned. Those who had embraced the religion of Govind did not fare much better than those who had adhered to their faith. As a rule they were from the class who had been forcibly converted to Mahomedanism by the Afghan, and the Sikhs despised them for having refused to die for their religion. Despite the strong democratic sentiment in the *misls,* which at first selected their chiefs, the position of sardar became hereditary in families. They seem to have drifted towards this just as the Guruship, which commenced as a democratic institution, became hereditary, thereby firmly establishing the Sikh religion. Political influence and power thus fell into the hands of a military aristocracy —an oligarchy based on republican principles. There were no wide distinctions between class and class. Powerful as was the influence of bold independent action which brought fame and rank, it was an influence which pervaded all, and in which none was too poor to share. Friendship or a distant relationship made the minor chief partake the feeling of his feudal superior, and he in his turn formed a link between the highest and his own humble dependants. Simplicity of habits was the habit of all. The owner of twenty acres was as proud and independent as he of hundreds, boasting the same descent and the same exclusive possession of arms and land. They wove into the interpretation of Govind's stern creed their own military characteristics. The articles of that creed nursed all the strength of national feeling, and evolved an individuality built upon traditions, the brotherhood bond of the *pahal*, and a common cause, resulting in a distinct type of mind, character, and physique. They became a select ruling race, self-confident and independent, the bone and sinew of the mass of the people. At the close of the eighteenth century the Sikh confederacies formed an unruly republic in which arms more than laws prevailed, and courage preferably to equity and justice was the virtue most valued and respected.

# CHAPTER VII.

## SARDAR RANJIT SINGH.

RANJIT SINGH'S family history is much the same as that of other sardars who rose in the eighteenth century from the ranks of the Jats. His ancestors with their village occupations alternated freebooting, which the oppressed peasantry had to practise to supplement the precarious subsistence they got from the soil, the long-continued exactions of the Mahomedan conquerors having reduced all to a dead level of poverty. The saying among them was that nothing was left for them except what was actually in their mouths. About the middle of the seventeenth century one of his forefathers, a quiet industrious man, took to preaching the religion of Nanak in his village and neighbourhood north of Lahore. His dying injunction to his young son was to study the holy book and become a Sikh. This he did towards the end of the century at Amritsar, on attaining the age of discretion, the time when the baptism of the *pahal* is administered. He was not of the peaceful disposition of his father, for on returning home he associated himself with a band of cattle-lifters, and on Guru Govind Singh's appeal to the Sikhs he went south to the scene of action, became the leader of his band, and won the reputation of being the boldest and most resolute of the fraternity in capturing the enemy's herds and bringing them away north. Becoming thereby a man of importance and some wealth, he was elected headman of his village. When he died in 1716 his eldest son promoted himself in the profession and became a gentleman of the highway, which, compared with cattle-lifting, was considered more honourable and lucrative. He was notorious for boldness, and amassed what in those times was looked on as riches. He joined a *misl* at the time of the first Afghan invasion in 1748, which by plundering the baggage and stragglers of the army secured much booty for its members. A wound in action led to his death in 1752, when his son Charat Singh, grandfather of Ranjit Singh, succeeded to his patrimony of three ploughs and a well, representing about thirty acres of land. He separated himself from the *misl* his father had joined, formed an independent band of 150 horsemen, and became a noted freebooter and guerilla leader during the stormy times of the repeated Afghan invasions. He took forcible possession of some villages, united with another successful leader like himself, and formed a *misl,* of which he became the active chief, calling it after the name of his native village. He next captured a town held by the Government troops, killed the commander, and carried away much plunder and munitions of war, then built a fort as his stronghold, which was attacked by the

Mahomedan Governor of Lahore, whom he defeated. His *misl* now became powerful, and its prestige attracted many recruits to his banner. On Ahmad Shah of Kabul retiring in 1767 after his final invasion, he followed him up, captured the fort of Rhotas and several Mahomedan towns, and occupied the country north of the Jhelum. He contributed much to the success of the Sikhs at this final struggle for ascendancy. When the dreaded Afghan king had gone the sardars took to fighting among themselves for power. His successes involved him in conflicts with rival *misls*, and he died in the field in 1774 while engaged in one of these contests. He left a large territory to his young son Maha Singh, then ten years old, whose mother assumed charge for him during his minority. Sikh ladies played an important part in the history of these warlike times. She ruled with vigour and diplomacy until her son, at the age of fifteen, cut his leading-strings and took the field at the head of his *misl*, to follow in his father's victorious steps. He extended his influence and possessions by invading a powerful Mahomedan tribe on the Chenab, then defeated another confederacy, and routed and humbled many rival sardars, showing himself brave, enterprising, and prudent beyond his years. Many influential independent chiefs joined him, attracted by his courage in action and military ability, qualities which were inherited by his son Ranjit Singh, who as a boy of twelve succeeded him at his death in 1792.

Ranjit Singh, the national hero of the Sikhs, was born in 1780, and at an early age was afflicted by virulent smallpox, which left him disfigured and with the loss of an eye. The one-eyed boy grew up short of stature, and as chief of a *misl* he seemed what might be called a "sport" among the stalwart Jats who surrounded him; but he early showed commanding spirit, ability, and military genius, which marked him as their superior in action, in intellect, diplomacy, and all the qualities which ensure success. When he first, as a boy of twelve, stood in his father's place everything was against him. He was beset by enemies, by doubtful friends, false allies, and open foes. No care had been bestowed on his education; the little he had was that of the camp, as he often accompanied his father in his expeditions. A regency composed of his mother and his father's minister ruled the confederacy in his name, but the guiding spirit in his interest was a Sikh lady to whose daughter he was affianced. She was one of the most artful and ambitious of her sex who ever figured in Sikh history, and became the ladder by which Ranjit Singh ascended to power: a masterful woman, the widow of a sardar—heir to a rival *misl* —killed while fighting against Maha Singh, she aimed, by bringing about a marriage alliance between her daughter and Ranjit Singh, to secure his support to her claims to the sardarship of the *misl* to which her husband would have succeeded. This she effected in a short time, and proved a valuable ally to her son-in-law. Under her counsel Ranjit Singh looked to alliances before he went to war. At the age of seventeen heredity asserted itself: he freed himself from the control of his guardians, and engaged in operations against the Mahomedan tribes and in defence of his mother-in-law's possessions, showing the marked ability of his bold father which had so impressed the sardars.

When the Shah of Kabul invaded the Punjab for the last time in 1798 he, to show his power, formed a coalition and proceeded to subdue distant tribes and exact tribute. He subsequently came in to pay his respects to the Shah, with the result, as has been related, of attracting his attention and gaining by diplomacy what he desired, the royal grant of the governorship of Lahore, which place he occupied in 1799, loyally aided by his astute mother-in-law. Firmly established there, he consolidated his possessions and made arrangements to secure his authority as governor of the capital. His success alarmed other *misls*, and a powerful coalition was formed in 1800 to wrest Lahore from him. He went out to meet the confederates, broke them up, seized the possessions of the most powerful, and defeated in detail his declared enemies in other parts of the country. A king had now appeared among the lions. Lahore was ever after left in his undisturbed possession. In the following year, 1801, he formally assumed the title of Maharaja, going through the Hindu equivalent of a coronation ceremony, proclaimed that he was now to be styled "Sarkar," signifying power and state, established a mint, and issued in token of sovereignty a coin in his name bearing the inscription, "Hospitality, the Sword, Victory, and Conquest unfailing from Guru Govind Singh to Nanak."

The Sikhs had now reached nationhood under an able king fully equipped with confidence and energy, who, by transforming the Khalsa into a territorial power, decided once and for all whether the Sikh or the Afghan was to rule the Punjab. Thus, after a hundred years of unflinching struggle, was fulfilled the prophecy of the martial Guru Govind Singh.

# CHAPTER VIII.

## MAHARAJA RANJIT SINGH.

There was still much land to be possessed, Pathan governors to be expelled, and independent Sikh *misls* to be subdued, before the young Maharaja became absolute master of the Punjab. Fortified by prestige, the belief of others in him, he proceeded by force and craft to effect this. One by one all fell under his absorbing sway. Equality among the sardars was a fundamental law of the Khalsa, but was now observed much as other laws enacting equality have ever been. The hour had come and with it the man, when it became necessary to establish a central authority for the organised unity of the State. The copartnery system had served its purpose while it was the policy to oppose the Mahomedan everywhere in the land, whether Moghul, Persian, or Afghan—the policy of a struggle for life; but the sardars, long accustomed to independent action, ill-brooked the change to Ranjit Singh's policy of a struggle for one-man power, and often in durbar an old chief would address him as "brother" and speak out his mind regarding the new order of Khalsa affairs. The Sikhs soon found in their Maharaja a master who could unite them, and under whom they grew into a coherent nation stretching from the Sutlej to the Khaibar, from Multan to Kashmir. Not till he had proved his superiority over the numerous chieftains, who with their feudal followers formed the force of the Khalsa, did the Sikhs rise to that political and military prominence in which we found them in 1838, when the tripartite alliance was made, which led to the first Afghan war, for the restoration of the Durrani kingdom of Kabul in the person of Shah Suja, who, with his brother

Shah Zaman, from whom Ranjit Singh wrested the Punjab, had by an ironical stroke of fate been driven out of Afghanistan to take refuge in the country which the Durranis had so often subdued. In the execution of his policy to abolish feudal tenures he not only annexed the possessions of actively hostile rivals, but exacted death duties on every occasion of a sardar dying, leaving only small estates for their families, sweeping the rest into his treasury. He created his own army, giving rank and commands to his partisans, and where any chiefs were left with territory and power instituted "man-rent" in the form of contingents of irregular troops at his disposal for service.

In 1803 the British captured Delhi from the Mahrattas, the one strong native power then left in India. Those who still kept the field were followed up by Lord Lake, who defeated them wherever they stood. He pursued Holkar, their chief, who fled to the Punjab with the remnants of his once powerful and numerous army in the hope of finding an ally in the Sikhs. In alarm at finding the Mahrattas and British in their midst, a "Guru Mata," or National Council of the Khalsa, was held at Amritsar for the last time. They decided to stand aloof, and Ranjit Singh acted as mediator. The Mahrattas sued for peace from the victorious Lake, renounced all their possessions and claims in Northern India, and the Sikhs agreed to have no further concern with them. What Ranjit Singh heard then from the Mahrattas, and what he saw of the disciplined strength of the British army, made a deep impression on him. He determined then and there to be at peace with the dreaded advancing Power. He knew his own weakness. He had yet to give complete unity to the scattered Sikh elements, so he proposed to Lord Lake, in order to maintain friendly relations, that the Sutlej river should be the boundary between Sikh and Briton ; but as the British Government had inaugurated a strict policy of non-interference north of Delhi, nothing then came of this.

In 1806 Ranjit Singh crossed the river with a large force to assert his power among the Malwa Sikhs, as those in the Cis-Sutlej states are called, on which the British strengthened their frontier post north of Delhi. Again in 1807 and 1808 he crossed in force, levying tribute as King of all the Sikhs. The Patiala and other chiefs were alarmed. They saw they must either submit to Ranjit Singh or seek the protection of the British. They unanimously declined to accept him as their overlord and threw themselves on the protection of the British, saying that they had always been more or less under the wing of whoever was master of Delhi. The policy of non-interference—of masterly inactivity—had now undergone a change. An English envoy was sent to Lahore armed with an ultimatum, to negotiate a treaty on the condition of the independence of the Malwa Sikhs, and the Sutlej as the boundary of the Maharaja's dominion, British troops at the same time advancing to that river. By right of conquest the British inherited the power formerly exercised by the Mahrattas in this region when in possession of Delhi. Ranjit Singh, seeing that the British were in earnest, prudently concluded a treaty, agreeing to withdraw his claims over the Cis-Sutlej states and to recognise the river as the eastern boundary of his kingdom. He feared that other independent chiefs in the Punjab might claim British protection and defeat his cherished plan of kingship. Thus was preserved the independence of the Sikh states, called the Phulkian, which exists at the present day.

The Phulkian *misl*, one of the most powerful of the original twelve Sikh confederacies, comprises the states of Patiala, Jhind, and Nabha. The founder was one Phul, a Jat of ancient lineage connected with Jesulmeer in the Rajputana desert, colonised by Jats who in the eleventh century migrated there from Multan, extending to Sirhind, about the same time that others of the tribe established themselves on the Jumna below Delhi, carving out the present Jat principalities of Bhurtpore and Dholpore. Phul built a village in 1640, calling it after his name. The Delhi emperor patronised him. He embraced the Sikh religion, and his seven sons became the ancestors of the reigning families of Patiala, Jhind, and Nabha. Other minor families sprang from them, all attaining to wealth and power. The chief of Patiala took the lead, and his successes over the Pathans and Rajputs brought many Sikhs from over the Sutlej to his banner. Ahmad Shah of Kabul, the conqueror of Delhi, to whom the Punjab was ceded by the Moghuls, made him Governor of Sirhind, with the title of Raja, later on investing his son with the insignia of an independent prince. Often the State was under the influence of women of courage, wisdom, and activity, who fought in person at the head of their troops. One of these Ranis in the field against the Mahrattas turned the fortune of the day by personal valour, drawing her sword and addressing her soldiers: "I have resolved not to retreat. It would be a shame for the Sikh nation if at this moment they left a woman, the sister of their sovereign, to be slain by their enemies." The British Government, by throwing its mantle over these states in 1809, saved them from the rapacity and absorbing power of Ranjit Singh; and they have ever since proved their gratitude by conspicuous attachment to their suzerain, markedly so in the darkest days of the great military revolt in 1857.

Though the Maharaja felt this check to his ambition, he soon brought his mind to see the great advantage which this treaty secured him. The Sutlej was a well-marked geographical as well as political frontier. He fully trusted the British. He knew he was safe in that quarter, so was now free to direct his whole force in other directions where he had yet many enemies to overcome, and to pursue his policy of reducing to subjection all sardars and Mahomedan chiefs within his kingdom having any pretensions to independence and power. Soon all the Sikh confederacies were swept away except the Ahluwalia, now represented by the Raja of Kapurthalla, who had gained the interest of the British Government by services rendered at the time Lord Lake drove the Mahrattas into the Punjab.

When the English envoy was at Amritsar in 1809 negotiating the treaty, his small military escort was attacked by a large body of the fanatical Akali Sikhs, who were completely routed by the few disciplined redcoats. Ranjit Singh witnessed this, apologised for the outrage, complimented the envoy on the bravery of his soldiers, and expressed his admiration of their steadiness. He realised the effect of their discipline as absolutely decisive against the courage and numbers of his own fiercest soldiers devoid of organisation. It was an object-lesson to him which decided him to train his army according to European methods. He commenced by means of some deserters from the Indian army to drill his men, and formed a few battalions of Sikhs, Hindostanis, and Gurkhas after the British model, adopting the red coat. The turbulent Sikhs at first resented the new order of things. He had great difficulty in inducing them to abandon their old weapons and mode of fighting, but with tact and patience won them over by good pay and rations, and by personal example in shouldering the musket himself, wearing the red coat, and drilling in the ranks under the instructors.

The Honourable Mountstuart Elphinstone, when returning in 1810 from a mission to the Durrani King of Afghanistan, gives an account of his first meeting with a detachment of Sikh soldiers of that day guarding the Indus frontier. Contrasted with the Afghan Court and army he found them very Goths in manners and habits, loud talking, boisterous, and addicted to drinking-bouts.

They were tall and muscular, wild-looking, with uncut beards and long hair, legs bare up to the thighs, wearing loose scarves thrown over one shoulder, armed with sword and shield, matchlock, spear, and also the bow and arrows of their forefathers, with which they were expert. Chiefs and men all sat down together to eat and drink on a footing of equality. They obeyed instructions, but there was little order. They were merely unruly guerillas.

Like other Indian princes who succeeded in raising their armies to any degree of efficiency, Ranjit Singh appreciated the value of European officers. In 1822 two French colonels arrived at Lahore by way of Persia in search of military employment, asking if they could render any service by their "knowledge of the art of war acquired as superior officers under the immediate command of the great Napoleon Bonaparte, Sovereign of France." They were told to write out their application in French, and this was sent to the English political officer at the frontier for translation. The Maharaja was satisfied, and took them into his service as generals. Two others followed who had also served in the Napoleonic wars, and were given the same rank. Eventually about twenty foreign officers of various nationalities were employed in the Sikh army, some of whom were now and then placed in charge of districts as governors. With their aid he put into execution his cherished design to convert his horde of horsemen into a trained regular army, and established arsenals for the manufacture of cannon, small-arms, ammunition, and military stores.

These European officers were handsomely paid, and enjoyed the confidence of the Maharaja, but were never consulted in affairs of State. The ablest and most important among them were the four French officers who first arrived—Generals Ventura, Allard, Court, and Avitabile. They held the commands of the strong trained divisions of infantry, artillery, and cavalry, the first in rank, equipment, and discipline, forming the old guard of the army on which Ranjit Singh relied for success. All were dismissed after his death during the anarchy which then prevailed, the sardars being jealous of their influence among the troops. Dr Wolff, the Eastern traveller, gives an amusing account of meeting one of these foreigners in Sikh employ. Arriving late one night at the town of Gujrat, he was taken to the governor's house, when to his surprise he heard some one singing "Yankee Doodle" with the true American tone. It was the governor himself! Wolff asked him how he came to know this pleasant song, and received the reply, "I am a free citizen of the United States, from the State of Pennsylvania, city of Philadelphia. I am the son of a Quaker. My name is Josiah Harlan." When roving in the Afghan border, he was captured by the Sikhs. Ranjit Singh, appreciating his talents, told him, "I will make you Governor of Gujrat, and give you 3000 rupees a-month. If you behave well I will increase your salary; if not, I will cut off your nose."

Enlistment in the trained Sikh army was quite voluntary, and once the objection to the changes introduced was overcome, the service was very popular, the men being picked from large numbers of candidates, which rendered the army capable of expansion in an emergency. He also incorporated in the ranks his various subjects, Dogra Rajputs and Punjabi Mahomedans. Opposing elements were useful to him on occasions. The pay was good, higher than in the Indian army, but no pensions were given. Special attention was paid to the training of infantry and artillery as the principal arms for pitched battles. Except in head- and foot-gear they were dressed and accoutred like the British, in red and blue, with regimental facings to distinguish corps. The organised cavalry, under a French general, were trained and uniformed as cuirassiers and dragoons *à la Français.*

In addition there was a large force of light troops in the form of irregular cavalry and infantry which certain chiefs had to furnish on requisition, all armed after their own fashion, the cavalry wearing chain-armour and steel helmets, round which they wound turbans—the helmets similar to those worn by the Parthians who overwhelmed the legions of Crassus, and by the soldiers of Saladin and Tymur.

Ranjit Singh's reign was one long campaign in consolidating his power. By 1831, after repeated attempts, he had at last brought into subjection the Mahomedan provinces of Multan, Kashmir, and Peshawar, the Rajput hill states, and all other independent chiefs. His supremacy extended to the foothills beyond the Indus, to Ladakh in Thibet beyond Kashmir, and to the snowy Himalayas in the north.

Shah Suja, the last of the Durrani dynasty, was driven out of Afghanistan in 1822, and the country was divided among the Barakzai chiefs (the present ruling house in

MAHARAJA RANJIT SINGH REVIEWING HIS ARMY.

Kabul), one of whom held Peshawar as a vassal of the Sikhs, while his brother, Amir Dost Mahomed, ruled Kabul—he who played such an important part against the British in the first Afghan war. He plotted to recover Peshawar. This decided Ranjit Singh in 1834 regularly to annex it. He met the Afghans under the Amir and forced them to retreat. When hotly pushing on to retrieve a check to his advanced troops, he boldly at much loss forded the Indus at the head of 15,000 cavalry, crossing his light guns on elephants, and swept through the valley. Another and last attempt was made in 1837 by the Afghans, led by the Amir, to recover Peshawar, when again they were defeated and retreated precipitately. Fierce and sanguinary were the struggles for the possession of the northern gate into the Punjab. There the Sikhs decisively overcame the Pathans in a deadly tug of war, and also stemmed the tide of Wahabi invasion so fraught with danger to India.

The occupation of Peshawar was Ranjit Singh's last campaign; it effectually sealed the solidarity of his power. There was now nothing more left in the Punjab for him to conquer, and he longed to extend his sway over the rich lands of Sindh south of Multan, for he was a conqueror at heart, animated to the end of his life with all the energy and fire of his early days of power. Being checkmated in this design by the British, he quietly controlled the hostile element at his Court, which urged him to action. On one of his sons, impelled by the war party, at a great parade imploring his father to let him lead the army against the English, the reply was, "No, my son; remember the two hundred thousand Mahratta spearmen who opposed the English; not one remains." Some of the old Sikh sardars, whose blood never ran cool enough for diplomacy, were very free now and then in expressing their ideas regarding his policy. A few years before, when the Jats of Bhurtpore, besieged by a British force, begged for his aid, which he refused, they, to mark their opinion of his conduct in not responding to the call of his kindred race, sent him a woman's garments; but it had no effect in his decision to abide by his treaty not to cross the Sutlej. His opinion of them was that although they were capable as generals they were incapable as "men of affairs." When the first Afghan war was decided on to eject Dost Mahomed and restore the Durrani kingdom, he joined in the alliance with the British against the wish of his sardars, who advocated independent Sikh action beyond Peshawar, but he adhered to his decision and faithfully performed his part.

He died in 1839, while the British army was in Afghanistan, but his policy was maintained by his sons to the close of the war, true to their father's trust. He never wavered in his loyalty to the treaty made by him in 1809 at a critical time in the history of the Sikh nation. From the first when he met the British, although he had

Holkar and the Mahrattas as refugees supplicating an alliance, and all Hindostan was in a blaze, he formed a clear conception of English strength and resources, and acquired a great respect for their character. Though a man of immense ambition, he was gifted with a far-sightedness that few Indian rulers have possessed, and one of the main lines of his policy was to keep his word with the British and avoid under all circumstances collision with them. To his death he remained with them on terms of implicit confidence and the utmost friendliness, and never ceased to impress on all around him to maintain this as they valued their independence; but that he had doubts in his mind as to what the future might bring was shown when, a short time before his death, on looking at a map of India, he asked why so much of it was coloured red, and being told it marked British territory, he said with a sigh, "It will soon be all red."

The only time when he ever apparently

showed any doubt of the good faith of the British was, as related by the French General Allard, on the occasion of his going to meet the Governor-General of India in 1831 on the banks of the Sutlej, a meeting which he desired politically in order to strengthen his status. Some of his sardars were very averse to this, fearing kidnapping, which as a recognised method of political action was not unknown among the Sikhs as well as in other countries in olden times. He however proceeded in state with a large force, encamping on his side of the river, the British camp being on the other. The night before he was to cross over to the British camp he suddenly changed his mind, having been again warned that he would act unwisely in leaving his own territory to meet the English on their ground; that it would be safer to have the meeting at Amritsar, or to postpone it altogether. He sent for his French General Allard to inform him that he would not attend the meeting next morning. Allard argued with him to allay his apprehensions, and offered to stake his head that nothing unpleasant would happen. The Court astrologers were summoned; after consulting their mystic books they declared that the British were his sincere friends, and that the meeting would lead to more valuable friendship between the two States, but they also advised him to hold an apple in each hand, and on meeting the Governor-General to offer him one of these, keeping the other himself. If it was accepted the meeting would be favourable, and the visit could be carried out without the least fear. The next morning, when he crossed mounted on an elephant surrounded by his sardars and escort of Allard's dragoons, on meeting Lord George Bentinck he presented the apple to him, which was at once accepted. Delighted at this good omen, he stepped from his howdah into that of the Governor-General and proceeded to the audience tent, vivacious and charming every one by his manners, full of inquiry about all he saw. It may be that this little comedy of nervous fear was played by the clever Maharaja to show his suspicious sardars how ignorant they were to judge of his English friends by themselves.

Seven years later, in 1838, he again went to meet the Governor-General at Ferozepore, where the British army was assembled prior to the invasion of Afghanistan. There was no opposition then from his sardars. On this occasion Lord Auckland in state made a return visit to the Maharaja at Amritsar, being received with great honour and cordiality. With his staff he accompanied his royal host to the sacred Golden Temple, where they sat side by side listening to an oration by the priest to the effect that the two potentates were brothers and friends, and never could be otherwise. He took his own line, determined to show how complete his confidence was, and, to the amazement of his ministers and sardars, and against their wishes, conducted his English friends over the fort of Govindgurh, kept carefully guarded and only opened to his personal order, where his treasures were stored, allowing all the officers of the British escort, and even the engineers, to inspect it. His people then said that they now saw Sikhs and Englishmen were "to be all of one family and to live in the same house." Afterwards at an evening entertainment he took up a yellow-red apple, remarking on its colours, the yellow the favourite colour of the Sikhs and the red that of England, blended together as a symbol of the alliance of the two kingdoms,—a fruit pleasant to look upon and solid to the core. The treaty of perpetual friendship was then renewed.

Ranjit Singh was a unique personality among the rude Jats of those times. Deficient in the physical characteristics that win respect from barbarians, yet by his personal bravery, ability, and address he drew all around him to his wishes. He knew when to execute, when to yield, and how to contract his measures. With a clear conception of the object in view, when it became necessary to secure it by force he ruthlessly employed every means to gain it, always "grasping his nettles." As a soldier, though he sacrificed his men with prodigality to win the day, yet he was carefully economical of their lives. They were devotedly attached to him, all feeling under his command the exhilarating effects of confident success. Generous to the vanquished, it never being his policy to reduce any one to desperation, there seems to have been no sentimental manifestations in his politics, as he would not allow to remain any remnants of hostile power enough to furnish the elements of revival — to stultify his main purpose of rendering rebellion impossible. Continuity was the essence of his policy. Though illiterate, he managed better than others more learned to transact the current duties of his state by means of his retentive memory, quickness of mind, and keen observation. The evolution of a monarchy was irresistible under his masterful action.

He was at home in the saddle and in

camp among his soldiers, taking his meals in their presence. Love of horses was a passion with him ; he procured the best at all costs from far and near, once even sending an army under his son and a French general to secure at an exorbitant price a celebrated one from his Pathan vassal at Peshawar. Possessing great powers of endurance, he was given to long journeys on horseback, surprise visits to distant parts of his dominions enabling him to check his governors in their reports as to revenue and other matters. His Court was brilliant with oriental pageantry, but personally he was free from pomp and show, and so scrupulously simple in his dress among his gorgeously clad sardars as to be distinguished among the distinguished ; yet all feared him. Notwithstanding his apparent insignificant appearance, at first sight in strong contrast to the stalwart chiefs about him, he at once impressed and charmed foreign visitors by his superior mind, frank manners, and speech.

Captain Burnes, the English envoy sent in 1831 with a letter and presents from King William IV. of England, writes of his reception, when he suddenly found himself in the arms and tight embrace of a "diminutive old-looking man," the great Maharaja Ranjit Singh: "I never quitted the presence of a native of India with such impressions as I left this man. Without education and without a guide he conducts all the affairs of his kingdom with surpassing energy and vigour, and yet he wields his power with a consideration quite unprecedented in an Indian prince." In conversation with him he praised the bravery of his Sikhs, to whom he acknowledged he owed his success; that they were devoted to their duty and free from prejudice; would in emergencies carry eight days' provisions on their backs, dig wells when water was scarce, build forts and construct roads. Jacquemont, the distinguished French oriental traveller, who visited him at Lahore, wrote of him as an extraordinary man, a

Bonaparte in miniature. "His conversation is like a nightmare. He is almost the first inquisitive Indian I have met, and his curiosity balances the apathy of his nation. He has asked me a hundred thousand questions about India, the British, Europe, Bonaparte, this world in general and the next, hell, Paradise, God, the devil, and a myriad of others of the same kind."

King and political head of the Punjab, as well as chief of the Khalsa, he aimed at reconciling the varied divisions of race and creed among his subjects by employing all in his service. He kept up, however, the theory of the Khalsa, attributing every success to the favour of the Guru in the name of the Lord. "God the helper—Ranjit Singh," was his sign-manual. The Sikhs retained special privileges as the ruling race, the heart and soul of the military nation—the favoured of the State. As landowners they were lightly assessed, while all others were heavily taxed. Much scope was given to their individual ambition, which maintained the independence of their character.

Many of the old orthodox Sikhs lamented his assumption of irresponsible power, which destroyed the theocratic Khalsa policy of preventing any one chief establishing absolute power; and they recalled the days of equality when he lived at Amritsar as one of themselves, though the first among the equals. They viewed with alarm his Court surroundings of men who were not Sikhs, who encouraged him to confine the Jats to the army as not clever enough for statecraft. The Brahmans and Dogra Rajput chiefs looked on them as inferiors, only fit as soldiers to obey their orders. Their object was to adopt the Mahratta policy—to combine the Sikh fighting power with their statesmanship. The rude Jat soldiery were eventually at the mercy of these intriguers. Govind Singh's warning against the class was forgotten. The Maharaja's religious tolerance was not agreeable to the old school, who reproached him for countenancing the presence of Hindu and Moslem ascetics at his Court, and departing from the doctrines of those who had shed their blood to found a purified faith. Clever Brahmans exercised influence over him during his last days to such an extent that at their instigation he resorted to the "pious tricks" for securing salvation denounced by Guru Govind Singh, by giving away to them to gain their prayers for him all his jewels, horses, and other personal valuables. He even willed away as a gift to the Hindu shrine of Juggarnath the great Koh-i-noor diamond, formerly taken from Delhi by Nadir Shah, and which had been extorted from Shah Suja of Kabul when he fled to Lahore; but the peerless gem was saved by the state treasurer refusing to pass it out for dedication, as he said it was Government property which should not be given away in alms. In this he was supported by the sardars, who associated its possession with the independence of the Sikh kingdom, it being a saying of the Maharaja's that whoever owned it would be the conqueror of the Punjab.

Ranjit Singh, the Lion of the Punjab as he was called, by courage, energy, promptness, and decision raised himself from the chiefship of a freebooting clan to be a king whose friendship was sought by distant sovereigns and princes. He undoubtedly saved the Sikhs from anarchy, disintegration, and sinking into insignificance by his masterly action in binding them together at a time when, persecution and common danger having disappeared, the confederacies were, like a loosely tied bundle of faggots, inimical to one another and intent on personal aggrandisement. The *misls* had done their work, and union was absolutely necessary to preserve their strength. As Nanak woke up the people by reforming their religion, and Govind by stern discipline developed their political independence, so Ranjit Singh, with a wise old head on his young shoulders, seizing the opportunity to found a military monarchy on the fruits of their labours, gave coherence to the Sikh nation. He was a great man of action and a good ruler for his time, his Government—a mild despotism—being then the only one suited to control the diverse and turbulent elements in the Punjab. Under his strong hand such order and security reigned there as had never been known before. He left to his successor (unfortunately a weak man) a united kingdom, a territory larger than the present Italy, and a well-appointed trained army provided with the best weapons of the day, which the British, a few years later, found the most difficult to overcome that they had ever met in India. When he died the Sikh power was at its zenith, and then it exploded, disappearing in fierce but fading flames.

# CHAPTER IX.

## DECLINE OF THE SIKH MONARCHY.

THE Sikh kingdom, built up by forty years of resolute ability, did not long survive its founder. Its vigorous life was summed up in the person of Ranjit Singh: he symbolised its unity; he spoke for it to his neighbours. Neither his wisdom nor masterly spirit was in any measure possessed by his successors. On the loss of his strong hand the State was torn asunder by dissensions between rival princes, ministers, queens, and sardars, and rapidly declined, until ten years later it fell by conquest to the British, on whom the Sikhs fatuously forced war. The Khalsa, the one united power left, became prætorian in character, selling their services to the highest bidder. Army delegates decided in Council the fate of king and country, making and unmaking their rulers and officers. Murder was to settle every claimant, whether as Maharaja or Wuzir. There is not to be found in the annals of any country a more blood-stained record of relentless struggles for power than that of this epoch in Sikh history, when three Maharajas, three Wuzirs, and other aspirants to power in quick succession met violent deaths.

Some time previous to his death Ranjit Singh had taken into special favour the family of his minister Raja Dhian Singh, a Dogra Rajput, consisting of his son and two brothers, upon all of whom he conferred the title of Raja with princely *jagirs* or fiefs for their maintenance. Poor, but of good family, they entered the Sikh service as troopers; handsome and well-mannered, they soon attracted notice by their ability, and rapidly rose to high positions, where their influence in public affairs became paramount; but not being Sikhs, they were looked on with great jealousy by the other sardars. They played a deep game in the intriguing policy of that time, bent on gaining power and wealth, and on becoming independent, a policy which ultimately was successful.

The Dogra Rajputs, a branch of the old Aryan invaders of India, survived the Mahomedan invasions by occupying the hilly country north of the Punjab plains, where they maintained their independence till conquered by Ranjit Singh. They held aloof from the Sikh movement, as one in which their high caste was disregarded. They are strict Hindus, very clannish, loyal to their chiefs, and good soldiers, with all the Rajput pride of ancient lineage, disdaining every service but that of arms.

Kharak Singh, eldest son of Ranjit Singh, succeeded as Maharaja in 1839. He was weak in character and incompetent as a ruler. Under the evil influence of a sycophant Court favourite, his father's minister was ignored and insulted, and a plan made to assassinate him; but this coming to his knowledge, he resolutely formed a coalition with Nao Nihal Singh, the Maharaja's only son, a capable youth of fiery temper, and some sardars, lineal descendants from a common ancestor with Ranjit, to depose Kharak, regarding whom a rumour had been set afloat that he contemplated submission to the British when the Sikh army would be disbanded. This powerfully appealed to the soldiery, who now looked on the Maharaja as a traitor to his country. The minister with his adherents entered the palace before sunrise, cut down the royal guards, penetrated to the private apartments, and killed the obnoxious favourite in the presence of his master. Kharak Singh was then deposed after a reign of three months, and his son Nao Nihal Singh placed on the throne.

The deposed Maharaja died the following year, not without suspicion of poisoning, and the son mysteriously met his death

PRINCE SHER SINGH—MAHARAJA OF THE PUNJAB, 1841-1843.

(SON OF MAHARAJA RANJIT SINGH.)

CLAD IN CHAIN ARMOUR AND STEEL HELMET WITH HERON PLUMES.

by what was called an accident while returning from his father's funeral obsequies. The designing minister now supported the queen-mother in her claim to govern as regent, on the ground that her deceased son's widow was *enceinte*. He also at the same time inspired Prince Sher Singh, a son of Ranjit Singh, to advance his claim to the throne. An armed contest commenced between the two claimants. The Prince appealed to the army, secured its aid by lavish promises, and made a dash at the capital, when the queen-mother with a Dogra force retired to the citadel and made a stout fight against overwhelming numbers, but had to capitulate after a five days' siege, during which time some thousands were killed and the city of Lahore plundered. The loss of her life soon afterwards followed her loss of power. The clever Dogra Rajas on this occasion actively participated on both sides and secured much wealth.

Sher Singh became Maharaja in 1841,

but intrigue being rampant in the army, his Government lost all control over it. The military administration was now conducted by *panchayats,* or Councils of five delegates from each company in each regiment elected by their comrades—a democratic mode of self-government common in India, in villages, guilds, and other bodies, —synonymous with "Vox populi, vox Dei," as according to the Indian saying, "God is in the *panchayat.*" These army councils formulated demands for increased pay and the dismissal of all officers obnoxious to them. On being refused they murdered many of their officers, sending them "aloft," according to their slang, and then plundered Lahore. The European officers had to flee. The mutiny extended to the provinces, and for some months all government was in abeyance, the soldiery being complete masters. At last, tired of their own excesses, they modified their requests, and tranquillity was restored. But from this time discipline and subordination ceased in the army; the soldiers, conscious of their power, cared little for any authority.

Maharaja Sher Singh on all occasions expressed himself favourable to the British, scrupulously adhering to his father's policy. It was solely owing to him that the British army, returning from Afghanistan in 1842, was allowed undisputed passage through the Punjab, many of the Sikh sardars being strongly disposed to attack it, as they thought the potent spell of victory so long attached to it had been broken at Kabul and by the policy of evacuating Afghanistan. His constancy exasperated the hostile party, of which the sardars who had taken part in deposing Kharak Singh were the active spirits, and they disputed Sher Singh's right to the throne as that of a reputed son only. They formed a plot to assassinate him. This was effected in 1843 while he was inspecting some cavalry on parade, and was followed by the murder of his son and heir and the rest of the family. The

Dogra minister was in the plot; but after the deed, while conferring with the conspirators as to the future form of government, he was killed in order to get rid of the ascendancy of the powerful Dogras. Then followed further bloodshed. His son Raja Heera Singh appealed to the army to avenge these murders, and inflamed the soldiers by asserting that unless they acted with him the British would seize the Punjab and disband them, when, he added, from the Rajput point of view, "The Sikhs who now took a pride in the profession of arms would be compelled to seek an ignoble living by following the plough." This, coupled with a promise to increase their pay by one-half, was enough for the soldiery, now masters of the government. They in great force attacked the conspirators, who had shut themselves up in the citadel, captured it, and extirpated them, Lahore being again sacked. The young Raja brought the head of his father's murderer to the widow, a noble

Rajputni dame, who was waiting by her husband's body. She then said, placing his father's warrior plume on the son's turban: "My mind is now at perfect ease. Let the funeral pyre be prepared, and I will follow my lord in his journey to the next world. When I see your father I will tell him you acted as a brave and dutiful son."

The assembled Councils decided to place on the throne Duleep Singh, a boy of ten, who had been tardily acknowledged as the youngest son of Ranjit Singh, with Raja Heera Singh as Wuzir. Again the army demanded concessions and also the dismissal of the European officers, all of which were complied with, their power being irresistible. A brother Raja of the murdered Wuzir appeared on the scene as a claimant for the wuzirship. He was killed in his attempt to supplant his nephew. Then two young princes, adopted sons of Ranjit Singh,—Kishmira Singh and Peshora Singh, so called after the conquest of Kashmir and Peshawar,—bade for power, instigated by the last of the three Dogra brother Rajas. Some of the old Khalsa chiefs, although hostile to the Dogra party, took the bait and supported the claimants, hoping thereby to get one of themselves made Wuzir. The Maharani Jindan, mother of Duleep Singh, cajoled them and temporised with the object of getting rid of all rivals. She feared and distrusted them all, and schemed so that the minister who had placed her son on the throne, under whose patronage she chafed, was killed, and her brother, Sardar Jowahir Singh, appointed in his place. In the conflicts and intrigues the two princes were treacherously slain. The rejoicings of the Court over this infuriated the army, with whom they were favourites as adopted sons of their old Maharaja, and they with some good reason ascribed their deaths to the new minister, being encouraged in this by the Dogra element. The Maharani was powerless in their hands: she bribed them, and even admitted the fact, recommending them to be quiet, as "there was no use in lamenting over those who were no longer among the living." They, however, swore to take vengeance on her brother as the author of the crime, and sent messages to him demanding his presence before them to answer the charge. He ignored them. They then insisted on the Maharani coming to the main camp of the army with the young Maharaja and the minister, on pain of seeing her son deposed. She very reluctantly obeyed the summons, being assured by one of her Court advisers, Lal Singh, a Brahman sardar, who had his own aims in view, that all would go well.

The State procession, escorted by the royal bodyguard, set out on the fateful visit,—the minister on an elephant holding in his arms the young Maharaja, the last of Ranjit Singh's acknowledged line, the queen-mother following in her golden howdah on another. As they approached the camp the Khalsa was assembled on parade; there was a strange quiet along the line. The Maharaja was received with royal honours, his mother making lavish promises as she passed on. On reaching the centre a Sikh soldier came forward and gave the order to halt. The military councils, deliberating on the right of the line, had decided that the minister was guilty of the murder of the two princes and was to be executed. Suddenly the bugles sounded and the drums beat; four battalions advanced, removed the escort to a distance, and surrounded the elephants of the *cortége*. Ten of the Council appeared; the minister was ordered to descend. He tried parleying: a soldier ascended to his howdah and removed the young Maharaja, who was placed in his mother's arms. She was escorted to a tent prepared for her, holding up her son and crying for mercy in his name for her brother. The doomed minister was then executed in full view of the army. A soldier mounted his elephant, calling out, "How dare you disobey the order of the Khalsa?" bayoneted him and flung him to the ground, where he was at once despatched with many wounds. The Maharani heard her brother's cry of pain, and, cursing the Khalsa, flung away in her grief and rage the boy Maharaja, who was caught by a soldier. Thus did the Khalsa, with wild justice and in memory of their beloved old chief, avenge the murder of the two princes. Next morning, after an agonised scene over her brother's body, the queen with her son was escorted back to the palace. This took place in September 1845. Inconsolable for many weeks after this tragedy, she became regent and managed her own ministerial duties, but she was determined to be revenged. This judicial murder of her brother became the direct factor in bringing about war with the British.

The power of the army was now at its height. The highest officers of the State dreaded it. There were no means of meeting its rapacity, as the treasury was empty.

Anarchy reigned everywhere, and no revenue was forthcoming from the distant provinces. Stimulated by these internal dangers, the Durbar sought relief in external adventure. War with the British was to be the remedy. Anti-British feeling ever since the death of the wise Ranjit Singh was the prevailing weapon used in political intrigues. The fire which had been so long played with now became master. The idea of the Maharani in her spirit of revenge was after that of Iago, "Whether Briton killed Sikh, or Sikh killed Briton, or each do kill one another, either way makes my gain." She feared the Sikhs far more than the British. If victorious, the Khalsa would be engaged in plundering India, and she would gain the credit; if not, she could depend upon the British for life and generosity. At her instigation Raja Lal Singh, a Brahman favourite, was made Wuzir, and another Brahman, Raja Tej Singh, appointed commander-in-chief. The Dogra Raja Gulab Singh, the last of the brothers who had taken such a prominent part in the policy of these revolutionary times, held aloof and left the Khalsa to its doom. He thirsted for revenge on them for having killed so many of his family, but kept his head, biding his time to carry out his cherished design of independence.

A council of sardars and military delegates was held in the end of November 1845 to discuss the situation, when it was urged that unless something was done the Sikh power would collapse, and, as often happens in such cases, the something was fatuous—namely, the tragic error of violating the treaty with the British. The army was swept into the vortex of intrigue. There was a unanimous cry for war, and they became importunate to be led against the British—to the plunder of India. Some of the old Sikh sardars were averse to this, but they were powerless against the Court and the insolence of the soldiery. War was then declared without a shadow of provocation, and the order issued for the army to prepare to march. Now came a lull in revolution and assassination — the calm before the storm. The Khalsa prepared for the war with enthusiasm. They would take Delhi, sack it to pay off old scores, plunder the other rich cities of India, march to Calcutta and even to London! They were as well armed as the British, and could bring on the ground a preponderating force of men and guns; an initial victory would certainly be theirs, and then they would be joined by the Sikh states across the Sutlej. Such were their boasts. The glamour was soon dispelled. Only the iron hand of a Ranjit Singh could then have saved them from rushing to their ruin, but there was no one of such a calibre among them now. The chief sardars had gained affluence and lost moral force; the army was venal; and the arrogant ignorant *punches,* the military councils, ruled the Khalsa, which, deprived of the guidance of the European officers whom they had discarded, dashed itself against the British ranks in fierce but unavailing efforts to overcome them.

# CHAPTER X.

## THE FIRST SIKH WAR WITH THE BRITISH, 1845-46.

On the 11th December 1845 the Khalsa, confident of victory in all its pride of strength, crossed the Sutlej with 60,000 men and over 100 guns, and proceeded to invest the British garrison in Ferozepore, cutting off its line of communication before reliable information had reached British headquarters of the movement. While the Sikhs were concentrating on their side of the river, the Government of India, cautious to a fault, loth from political reasons to precipitate a collision, took no steps to strengthen their frontier posts of Ferozepore and Ludhiana beyond being ready to move up troops in case of actual aggression. These two posts, eighty miles apart, were each held by a division numbering between them 12,000 men and 36 guns, while at Amballa, 160 miles distant from Ferozepore, there was another strong division in support, the intervening country being practically roadless with a scanty water-supply. The enemy's plan of campaign was to cut off the British troops in detail by intercepting those coming up from the rear. Ferozepore, their objective, was the nearest point to their base and the farthest from British support.

Sir Henry Hardinge, the Governor-General of India, then in camp near Ludhiana, on hearing of the invasion of British territory declared war, and Sir Hugh Gough, Commander-in-Chief, marched on the 12th with the Amballa division, effected a junction on the way with that from Ludhiana, and by forced marches reached Moodkee, twenty miles distant from Ferozepore, on the 18th. On hearing of their approach the Sikhs moved out with 30,000 men and 40 guns to fall on them, hoping to fight only one division, but found that as the result of magnificent marching they were faced by two, numbering 11,000 men and 42 guns. This force had just concluded a long tedious march over sandy tracks when the information was received that the enemy was advancing in strength. They rapidly prepared for action at 4 P.M. The Sikhs took up a strong position among low sandhills in bush jungle and opened fire. The British horse artillery and cavalry vigorously assailed them in flank, and sweeping along their rear routed their cavalry, while they were attacked in front by the field-guns supporting the infantry, which, charging with the bayonet, drove them from position after position with great slaughter, and captured 17 guns. The Sikhs fought fiercely and retired sullenly in good order, seizing every opportunity to turn on their foes. Night only saved them from worse disaster. They retreated in the darkness to their main camp at Ferozeshah, ten miles off, which was strongly intrenched. They had tasted of British resolution and steel, and knew what to expect. They now laboured night and day to further strengthen their position, which consisted of a parallelogram one mile long by half a mile broad, surrounded by a ditch and earthworks ten feet high.

Reinforcements having reached the British army on the 19th, it was decided to follow up the victory of Moodkee by an immediate attack on this formidable work. Delay was dangerous; no further reinforcements could arrive for some time, and a decisive blow had to be struck to keep the protected Sikh states true to their allegiance. The invested Ferozepore division by a masterly movement effected a junction with the Commander-in-Chief near the enemy's work at Ferozeshah on the afternoon of the 21st, bringing his force up to 17,000 men and 69 guns; and although there only remained three hours to sunset and the troops had been marching since early morning, it was resolved to deliver the assault at once. In the words of the despatch, "a very heavy cannonade was opened by the enemy, who had dispersed over the position upwards of 100 guns, more than 40 of which were of battering calibre. These kept up a heavy and well-directed fire, which the practice from our far less numerous artillery of much lighter metal checked in some degree but could not silence; finally in the face of a storm of shot and shell our infantry advanced and carried these formidable intrenchments: they threw themselves upon the guns with matchless gallantry, and wrested them from the enemy; but when the batteries were partially within our grasp our soldiery had to face such a fire of musketry from the Sikh infantry arrayed behind their guns, that in spite of the most heroic efforts a portion only of the intrenchments could be carried. Night fell while the conflict was everywhere raging." The British attack on the left was repulsed, but a firm foothold was secured in the centre and right, despite fierce hand-to-hand fighting, when again and again the Sikh batteries were charged and the gunners bayoneted. The reserve division was brought up. "The

3rd Light Dragoons with a troop of horse artillery charged over the intrenchments, cutting down the gunners of some batteries which still kept up their deadly showers, dashed among the infantry and swept through the Sikh camp; yet the brave dogged enemy remained in possession of a considerable portion of the position, whilst our troops, mingled with theirs, kept possession of the remainder and bivouacked upon it, wellnigh exhausted by their gallant struggles, greatly reduced in numbers, and suffering severely from thirst and intense cold, but still animated with an indomitable spirit. In this state of things the long night (the longest in the year) wore away."

The Governor-General, General Sir Henry Hardinge, a Peninsula veteran, who chivalrously served with the army as second in command, in a letter to Sir Robert Peel, the Prime Minister of the day, graphically described the situation: "The night of the 21st was the most extraordinary of my life. I bivouacked with the men without food or covering, and our nights are very cold—a burning camp in our front, our brave fellows lying down under a heavy cannonade, which continued during the whole night—mixed with the wild cry of the Sikhs our English hurrah, the tramp of men, and the groans of the dying. In this state, with a handful of men who had carried the batteries the night before, I remained till morning, taking very short intervals of rest by lying down with various regiments in succession to ascertain their temper and revive their spirits. I found myself again with my old friends of the 29th, 31st, 50th, and 9th (regiments which had served in the Peninsula), all in good heart. My answer to all and every man was that we must fight it out, attack the enemy vigorously at daybreak, beat him, or die honourably in the field. When morning broke we went at it in true English style." Headed by Sir Henry Hardinge and Sir Hugh Gough, the infantry in line, supported by horse artillery, advanced steadily, unchecked by the enemy's fire, without a halt, from one end of the Sikh camp to the other, capturing more guns as they went along, which were served obstinately to the last, and dislodging the enemy from the whole position. The line then halted "as if on a day of manœuvre," receiving their leaders as they rode down its front with a hearty cheer, and displaying the captured standards of the Khalsa army, which was now in full retreat to the Sutlej, having lost 73 guns and several thousands of their numbers, and abandoned all their camp equipage and stores. The great object of checking the advance of the Sikhs had been accomplished by invincible energy and unbending determination.

The British casualties in these two actions of the 18th and 21st December amounted to about one-fifth of their number, the English troops suffering most in proportion, as the enemy specially directed their fire on them. Generally they lost about one-third of their strength, exceeding that of many hard-fought battles in Spain, in which some of the corps engaged had taken part. The loss of the Sikhs was never accurately known, but it was estimated at from 5000 to 8000, the number of guns captured being 90.

The battle of Ferozeshah was one of the most momentous, and certainly the hardest fought-out one, ever engaged in by the British in India. It has been said that the Sikhs then shook our Indian Empire to its base: the British soldiers, however,—true pillars of the Empire,—animated with all their prestige and pride of race, were strong and firmly rooted enough to stand the shock and uphold the fabric. The enemy were attacked at a late hour in the day when their force was divided, one portion being then still engaged in watching Ferozepore (probably intent on its plunder), where a small body of British was left intrenched, while the main portion, realising from their Moodkee experience the danger of fighting in the open, remained on the defensive within their earthworks, which they were actively engaged in strengthening. The British leaders knew the danger of even one night's delay, which might bring fatal consequences; a battle at once was absolutely necessary. They were obliged to be the assailants, and thus to incur heavy loss at the commencement; but they relied on the bravery and discipline of their men to make amends for disadvantages, and well were they justified. They had confidence in themselves and in one another; their disparity in numbers only made them act as if every man felt that the result depended on his own single conduct. They were conscious of their instinctive soldiership at close quarters and inspired with unbounded audacity. The attacking brigades were formed of an English regiment in the centre with a native one on each flank: the white-capped English corps formed the steel head of the lances which penetrated the Sikh works, marking out the path for their native comrades, hence their greater loss from the brunt of the fighting falling on them.

After Ferozeshah the British force took up positions near the Sutlej, and there awaited the reinforcements of all arms which were now moving up from India, preparatory to advancing on Lahore. The Sikhs rallied on the right bank of the river and commenced energetically to prepare to renew the contest. Though twice sorely defeated they were not subdued; they were yet destined to suffer on other "stricken fields" before they were left without excuse for defeat — without hope of recovery. With large bodies of well-trained old soldiers who joined them, and a fresh supply of guns from their arsenals, they became almost as strong as before. Under the direction of a Spanish officer they threw up batteries and extensive earthworks on both banks in a skilfully chosen position at a loop of the river, connected by a bridge of boats and a ford. Having lost all their great store of food-supplies their army delegates were sent to Lahore to demand more from the Durbar, as they were starving, and also to induce the Dogra Raja Gulab Singh to join them with his Dogra troops. They offered to make him Wuzir though not a Sikh, and to despatch their Brahman leaders, whom they distrusted; but he thought of himself, of his slain brothers and sons, and of the fickle Khalsa. He had undertaken the office of Minister after the defeat of Ferozeshah, and opened negotiations for peace; but when told the first demand of the British Government was the immediate disbandment of the Sikh army, he declared he was helpless to effect it, as he could not deal with the turbulent soldiery. He now cajoled the deputies, temporised, and collected supplies. The Maharani, however, was getting desperate; the Khalsa was on her nerves; she was in terror at the thought of their returning. She with the little Maharaja Duleep Singh received the deputation in Durbar, and heard their appeal. She upbraided them as cowards, took off part of her dress and threw it among them, saying, "This is your dress. Remain at home; I will go and fight." The resolve to get them destroyed was known to them, but such was the stern democratic discipline of their army councils, such their devotion to their warlike faith, that determination even now animated every man. They fiercely reproached her and her courtiers. Addressing the Maharaja, they said, "We will go and die for you, your kingdom, and the Khalsaji"; but to the others who had incited them to war and now taunted them with their folly in hoping to vanquish the conquerors of Hindostan, "We will leave you to answer to your God and your Guru, while we, deserted and betrayed as we are, will do what we can to preserve the independence of our country."

From this time on the Sikhs fought with doom against them. They now made a further effort upon the Upper Sutlej, which they crossed with 15,000 men and 67 guns to invest Ludhiana and cut off its communications. They met with some slight success at first, but a British force of 11,000 men and 32 guns sent from headquarters camp and Amballa having concentrated in that quarter relieved Ludhiana, and attacked the enemy at Aliwal on the 28th January 1846, signally defeating them, capturing their guns, and driving them over the river with severe loss. The Sikhs took up a strong semicircular position, within which was the village of Aliwal, their flanks resting on the Sutlej. In front lay open undulating hard grass-land; some manœuvring took place on both sides previous to the action. The local conditions were ideal for a set battle as a trial of strength. "There was no dust; the sun shone brightly, and the manœuvres were performed with the celerity and precision of the most correct field-day and with all the pomp of war." The enemy opened artillery-fire from his whole line upon the advancing British, who, throwing forward their right, captured at the point of the bayonet the village of Aliwal on the left of the position. The whole line then advanced and the battle became general; the British cavalry on the right flank charging that of the Sikhs, driving them on to their infantry, while the British infantry attacking in front drove everything before it, capturing battery after battery. The enemy, driven back on his left and centre, held on to a village on his right covering the passage of the river. There stood Avitabele's French brigade, so called from its organiser, 4000 strong with guns—the *élite* of the Sikh army. The 16th Lancers charged right through a square of their infantry, wheeling about and re-entering it to finish it off with the deadly lance. The Sikhs fought fiercely and with much resolution, maintaining hand-to-hand fighting. In one charge of their infantry upon the lancers they threw down their muskets and came on sword and shield in hand, after the manner of the Scottish clansmen, who were wont, when the decisive moment arrived, to drop their firelocks, draw their claymores, and rush upon the English dragoons. The British infantry concentrated upon the village held, carried it and the guns there, the remnants of Avitabele's brigade being driven to the river. The enemy, completely hemmed in, precipitated themselves in disordered masses into the boats and ford, while horse artillery galloping up committed great havoc among them. The *débris* of the Sikh force appeared on the opposite bank in full flight to their base position there. Fifty-six guns were taken and the rest sunk in the river. The victory was complete. The conquerors fired a royal salute in its honour, which was repeated by the vanquished on the other side as their *au revoir*. The Sikh camp at Sobraon was soon made aware of the defeat by the sight of the many dead floating down the river.

## CHAPTER XI.

### THE FIRST SIKH WAR—*continued.*

THE British troops now concentrated for the decisive struggle at Sobraon. On the 10th February 1846 the Sikh position there was attacked by a force of 15,000 men and 60 guns. They took up their station for close action during a dense fog which clung over the ground; when it rolled away under the rising sun the guns opened fire on the enemy's long line of strong intrenchments held by 35,000 men and 70 guns, mostly heavy, with a reserve in a strong position on the opposite bank of the Sutlej; the Sikhs, on the alert, returned the fire steadily. After three hours' cannonading the order was given for the infantry to storm the works. On this, as a regimental historian has it, "wild and long was the shout as, amidst showers of grape and musketry, they dashed forward towards the ramparts of clay and wood, upwards of ten feet high, where nothing appeared to view but the muzzles of the guns, behind which the Sikh infantry, four deep, were lining the intrenchments." Though driven back by superior numbers to take shelter in the ravines and folds of the ground, they leapt forward again and again at the call of their regimental leaders, till they gained a footing by shouldering one another up to the embrasures, capturing and spiking the guns in their front. The Sikhs fought stubbornly and desperately hand to hand, till at last the assailants, swarming through the breaches, mounted the ramparts with cheers of victory and took the whole line of intrenchments; but not till the weight of all the three divisions, all the cavalry, and the fire of every gun was felt did the Sikhs give way. They slowly retired in good order under cover of interior works, harassed by in-

REGULAR AND IRREGULAR INFANTRY—SIKH ARMY, 1845.

cessant volleys of musketry; but no Sikh offered to submit—no disciple of Govind asked for quarter. Everywhere they showed a bold front to the victors, whilst many rushed singly forth to meet assured death. Step by step they were forced back to the bridge of boats, which gave way under the pressure. The river had suddenly risen seven feet during the night, making the ford impassable. In the crowd many of their mounted officers, grey-bearded old chiefs, scorning to save themselves, were seen waving their swords on high, calling on their men to drive back the English, to vindicate their honour or die. Their heroic efforts to retrieve the day were of no avail; destruction awaited them on every side. The horse artillery coming up poured in a hot fire among them; terrible was the carnage, and thousands were drowned attempting to swim across. The Khalsa was disastrously routed; 67 cannon, 200 swivel guns, numerous standards, and vast munitions of war were the spoils of victory. Sir Henry Hardinge referred to it as "one of the most daring ever achieved, by which in open day a triple line of breastworks, flanked by formidable redoubts, bristling with guns, manned by thirty-two regular regiments of infantry, were assaulted and carried."

The British loss was 2400 killed and wounded,—about one-sixth of their force engaged,—that of the Sikhs in killed, wounded, and drowned being estimated at 10,000. Some of the English regiments, on whom the brunt of the fighting fell, lost one-third of their strength.

On the following day a party of Sikhs came in with a request to take away the bodies of their slain chiefs, among them that of Sardar Sham Singh, whose death they all deplored, a comrade of Ranjit Singh and an experienced and gallant old soldier. He had opposed the ill-fated cry of war against the British, but, unheeded in Council, threw in his lot with the Khalsa when the die was cast, and at the head of his men joined the army. At Sobraon he announced his determination not to survive another defeat, which he feared more than death. Dressed in white clothes, he was, with his long flowing white beard, conspicuous on the ramparts cheering on his ardent followers, directing the gunners where to fire on the English soldiers, confident, if they were destroyed, the day was gained. He fell honoured by his gallant opponents. His wife, a high-spirited Sikh dame, on hearing at her home of the defeat of the Khalsa, without waiting for details, immolated herself on the funeral pyre, as she said she knew her lord was dead, he having assured her he would not disgrace his family by returning defeated.

On the night of the victory at Sobraon advanced brigades were pushed across the river, and by the 13th the whole force was over and marching to the capital, which was reached without opposition within a week. The shattered remnant of the Sikh army retired and halted near Lahore, ready to lay down their arms. Within the short period of sixty days from the time when the Sikhs crossed the Sutlej so confident of victory, the British force, far inferior in numbers of men and guns, but superior in everything which makes for success, had defeated the flower of the great Khalsa in four well-fought-out pitched battles and wrested from them in action 220 guns, while only 14,000 of that derelict army now remained in the field. The much-plundered city of Lahore was amazed to find that it was spared from pillage, and to hear that the British had committed no outrages during their victorious march and scrupulously paid for everything they took. There was now nothing left to encourage the Sikhs to continue the contest; they had been well and fairly beaten, but they had forgot nothing of their prætorian pride. Their vanity was mortally wounded, so they raised the cry of treachery and turned on their Brahman leaders, to whom they ascribed all their disasters. They had, however, learned a good deal and unlearned much regarding the British; but, as was shown later on, they were not yet subdued, although they had found out that it was not bravery, of which they had plenty, nor numbers and good arms alone, that made a successful army, but also good generals and good leaders. An old Sikh soldier remarked to an English officer after the battle, "If we only had had your sahibs [officers] to lead and direct us in the way they did your soldiers, there would have been another story to tell."

The Prime Minister, Sir Robert Peel, in the House of Commons, when proposing the thanks of Parliament to the Indian Army of the Sutlej, spoke enthusiastically of their victories, interrupted by no single failure, —unsullied by any imputations on our arms or character,—and quoted from a letter to him the generous tribute of their brave veteran chief to the gallant foe: "Policy precluded me from publicly recording my sentiments on the splendid gallantry of our fallen foe, or to record the acts of heroism displayed not only individually but almost collectively by the Sikh sardars and army; and I declare, were it not from a deep conviction that my country's good demanded the sacrifice, I could have wept to witness the fearful slaughter of so devoted a body of men."

The Sikh army—the weapon which Ranjit Singh had so well forged—turned against his best friends, the British, who met in it the hardest fighting enemy they had encountered in the East, and whose gallantry and steadiness in action excited the admiration of their opponents just as that of their remote ancestors the Getæ or Indo-Scythic warriors at Arbela, twenty-two centuries before, when fighting under Darius against the Macedonian phalanx, drew forth the praise of the great Alexander. The names of Moodkee, Ferozeshah, Aliwal, and Sobraon have rung in history. A great tradition connected with the rise of our Indian Empire hovers round them, immortalising the unsurpassed example of unflinching courage set by the British soldier. They are emblazoned alongside other glorious battle-scrolls on the colours of the distinguished regiments who so nobly maintained on the banks of the Sutlej the high reputation of those before them in building up England's power.

Ranjit Singh's star set in red anarchy. Anti-British feeling ever since his death prevailed as the remedy to distract the Khalsa. The moment they thought was favourable to take the fatal step to occupy the Cis-Sutlej Sikh states, to rally their population to the blood-and-plunder cry. The British were nearly caught by their own unwillingness to move—to believe that the Khalsa was in earnest. Dilatory measures to move up troops to meet the menace being deemed expedient by the political authorities, the strong men armed were within our gates when the assembly sounded; but hard marching, and the devotion of the British soldier in response to Gough's stern appeal to close with the enemy, saved the situation. He stood eye to eye in front of an active strong power having greater elements at his back and in our own territory. The Sikh giant commenced the fight by delivering with his fist a solid blow full in the Briton's face. It was quickly and strongly returned, and he was grievously worsted. The problem Sir Hugh Gough had to deal with was to confine the war to the banks of the Sutlej. It was more of a soldier's war than a general's. He did not attempt to bring off strategical movements in the nature of evading the enemy, to fall on him unawares or force him to shift his ground to fight. He had few but very good troops. Support was far off; his main object was to meet the enemy and fight,—the harder the fighting the better, in order by bold tactics to shorten the war,—and he succeeded. At every stage he was greatly outnumbered; he saw that a stubborn foe behind works was not to be beaten down by his own inferior gun-fire, their guns being far more numerous, heavier, and well served. The keynote of his tactics was a bold intrepid charge — close quarters and the bayonet—to impress the enemy by audacity and daring. He clung with bulldog tenacity to the Sikhs after Ferozeshah, rejecting proposals to harry their rear over the river, waiting to deal a final knock-out blow when his force was refreshed, so as to leave farther advance unopposed. After this had been done our friends in rear and ahead were as thick as flies in summer. He was essentially a fighting general, a hard hitter, whose maxim was "L'audace, toujours l'audace." He grasped success. The generals, among them veterans of the Peninsula, Waterloo, and Afghanistan, were first and foremost in the thick of battle, exposing their lives freely and rousing the daring of their men to the utmost by personal example, several of them falling "in the rapture of the strife," cheering on to victory. With a small determined force it was the only decisive form of conducting the campaign, and every one was inspired by the direct spirit of their gallant chief. It made a great impression on the Sikhs, who would have extended the area of operations had strategical manœuvring been resorted to. They found that, whether in the open field or behind formidable works, they had met more than their match.

Immediately after the crushing defeat at Sobraon, the Lahore durbar, with all the Sikh sardars and army delegates, sued for peace on any terms, and the young Maharaja, with Raja Gulab Singh, came into the British camp to submit in the name of his Government. The work of the soldier having been completed and the enemy made amenable to reason at the point of the bayonet, a thick velvet glove was now put on the iron hand and generous terms dictated. By a treaty ratified in March 1846 the Maharaja was restored to the throne, the country between the Sutlej and Bias rivers ceded to the British, and a war indemnity of one and a half millions sterling imposed;

but as this amount was not forthcoming from an empty treasury, the hill country north of the plains of the Punjab was also ceded as an equivalent for one million. The regular army of the Lahore State was not to exceed twenty-five infantry battalions with 12,000 cavalry, to be paid and organised under the system which existed in the time of Ranjit Singh, the guns remaining in the arsenal being left to them. 250 guns, including all that had been pointed against the British, were marched off to Calcutta under escort, to be seen by all India as the spoils of battle and victory.

At the urgent request of the Durbar, who feared the disbanded Khalsa army, a British force of 10,000 men was left till the close of the year for the protection of the Maharaja and the city of Lahore, pending reorganisation of the Government and their army, which time was afterwards, on a special appeal signed by fifty-two of the chief sardars, by a new treaty in December 1846, extended reluctantly by the Governor-General until the Maharaja should attain his majority in 1854. The British Government invested the Dogra Raja Gulab Singh with the title of Maharaja, and in consideration of his paying out of his wealth, amassed during the troublous times, one million sterling of the war indemnity for the impoverished Durbar, Kashmir with its dependencies was transferred to him as independent ruler and vassal of the British—a very bad bargain for the Government, which unfortunately was rendered necessary by the political exigency of the moment. He, however, now reaped what he had sown by craft, and attained the object of all the diplomacy and bloodshed of his family since the death of his patron Ranjit Singh. The Maharani Jindan was acknowledged as queen-regent of the state, with her minion Raja Lal Singh as executive minister, and Major Henry Lawrence was left in charge of political affairs at Lahore with a voice in the Durbar.

# CHAPTER XII.

## THE SECOND SIKH WAR, 1848-49—ANNEXATION, 1849.

The policy of maintaining the Sikh kingdom was considered highly important, but the attempt to govern by a British protectorate broke down after a fair trial. The evil seeds of disintegration were in the Sikhs themselves. The Durbar was corrupt, weak, and divided against itself. Before the year was out the minister Lal Singh was caught red-handed in treachery. After the order was issued for the transfer of Kashmir to Maharaja Golab Singh according to the treaty, he sent letters to the governor there to resist this by force. Several conflicts ensued; and not till Colonel Henry Lawrence proceeded there, at the head of a body of Sikh troops who had been so lately fighting against us, was the transfer effected. Lal Singh was proved guilty by the production of his own letters; not a voice was raised for him, and he was banished to his native land in Hindostan.

A Council of Regency of the principal chiefs was now formed under the direction of the British Resident; but at the Lahore Court the witches' caldron, brimful with intrigue, again began to bubble. The queen-regent had hoped that everything except the dread Khalsa would have been restored to her as before the war. She bitterly resented the expulsion of her favourite minister, the arch-traitor Lal Singh, and after a short time the sardars also came to repent of the treaty they had made. Faithlessness to the too merciful British Government was encouraged; an army and guns still remained to them; disaffection was excited among the soldiery and the disbanded Khalsa, who swarmed, discontented, in the villages. The new wine, in the form of English officers sent by the Regency Council to various parts of the country to see orders obeyed, burst the old bottles of Sikh government, which had so long held methods of barbarism. The climax came in April 1848, when the reformed Durbar was forced to interfere with Mul Raj, the rapacious Hindu Governor of Multan, whose tyranny could not be tolerated under the eye of the British protectorate. He resigned, and a Sikh sardar was sent to relieve him, accompanied by two English officers — Mr Vans Agnew of the Civil Service and Lieutenant Anderson, with an escort of Durbar troops —to see him installed. They were treacherously wounded while returning from the fort with Mul Raj on his giving over the keys, and shortly afterwards murdered by some of his soldiers. Only the new Sikh Governor, his son, a few faithful horsemen, and some servants remained with them to the end, the escort having gone over to the enemy. They scorned to wave the white sheet of submission, Vans Agnew saying: "The time for mercy has gone; let none be asked for. They can kill us two if they like, but we are not the last of the English. Thousands of Englishmen will come here after we are gone and annihilate Mul Raj and his soldiers and his fort." The loyal Sikh sardar Kahan Singh and his son were imprisoned, and taunted with showing sympathy for the foreigners. When the fort was ultimately captured by the British, their dead bodies were found in the ruins of their prison clasped in one another's arms.

Mul Raj declared war against the British, and, gathering a force of some thousands, put his fort in a state of defence by making a deep ditch lined with masonry round a wall thirty feet high. Great importance was attached to the possession of this celebrated old stronghold for which so many battles had been fought in ancient and modern times — the scene of one of the great Alexander's exploits on his march down the Indus valley, where, leading the victorious Greek assault, he was severely wounded. The Mahomedan tribes in the neighbourhood had no love for the Sikh rule. They rallied to the summons of a young English officer, Lieutenant Edwardes, then in charge of the Derajat frontier, and twice sorely defeated the rebels, shutting them up in the city and fort. Sardar Sher Singh, one of the Court of Regency, sent down with 12,000 men and 12 guns, joined Edwardes; but they were unreliable.

The very hot summer was on in that hottest of hot localities in the Punjab; the proceedings of the Durbar were dilatory, and when told by the British Resident that the rebellion must be put down they professed their inability to undertake the task. A division of British troops was then sent: they reached the scene in August, when after some severe fighting they found the fort too strong to be successfully attacked, and took up a position awaiting reinforcements. Sher Singh with his Sikh force went over to the enemy in September, and before the end of the month left them, marching away north to join his father, Sardar Chutter Singh, the Sikh Governor of Hazara, who in August had revolted with all his troops. Not till December, when the British force at Multan was joined by a division from Bombay, was the siege vigorously resumed, ending by the capture of the city and surrender of the fort on 22nd January 1849, after a loss by them of 1200 killed and wounded. The bodies of the two murdered English officers were then taken from their neglected grave, wrapped in Kashmir shawls, carried up through the breach by the thousands of their countrymen who had come to avenge their death, and buried with military honours on the summit of the citadel.

The delay before Multan changed a local *émeute* into the rebellion of the whole Sikh nation, which now rose to re-establish the supremacy of the Khalsa and shake off the hold of the British, thinking that as they had abandoned Kabul some years before, so they would march out of the Punjab. The Maharani had not been idle at Lahore; she was mixed up with intrigues which demanded the sternest measures against the ringleaders, one of them being her confidential adviser: she was banished to India. Overtures for aid had been made by Mul Raj and the Sikh sardars to the Amir Dost Mahomed, the price being the cession of Peshawar, the province which Ranjit Singh had won from the Afghans, and for which his best had so freely shed their blood. The Amir marched there and sent his son with a contingent of Afghan troops to join the Sikh army,—an unnatural alliance between hereditary enemies, which drowned for a time creed antipathies. The Durbar troops at Peshawar now revolted and joined the rebels.

Sher Singh with his troops took up a position on the Chenab river, where the Khalsa in their thousands joined him. The Punjab was now aflame; the trumpet again spoke to the cannon, and the sound of battle rolled through the land. A rising took place of discontented leaders in the ceded districts, of which John Lawrence was Commissioner. The rebels proclaimed that the English rule had ceased. They were on the flank of the British army advancing from Lahore. Lawrence, with the genius of a born general, was promptly on the spot with a small force and some raw levies. "If you will excite rebellion, as I live I will severely punish you," was his dictum. He made short work of them, and then offered the people the choice between the sword and the pen as the instrument by which they wished to be ruled, —between enforced submission or willing obedience. His pen was grasped with enthusiasm, and the sword was sheathed and kept in reserve.

The Sikhs held the fords of the Chenab river and threw up strong works at Ramnugger on both banks to oppose the advance of the British under Lord Gough.

After severe fighting there and some desultory operations elsewhere, the passage was effected, and by the end of December all the British force had crossed to the north bank to drive the enemy towards the Jhelum and hold him in check, while waiting for the fall of Multan to set free more troops to join it.

Sher Singh showed considerable generalship in handling his army, now about 40,000 strong with over 60 guns. He took up a well-chosen position near the Jhelum, close to the classic field of Alexander's great battle with Porus in 327 B.C., and as the revolted Sikh troops were now marching from Peshawar to join him, Lord Gough determined to engage before they arrived. On the 13th January 1849 he advanced with 15,000 men and 66 guns to Chillianwala, where he drove in their advanced outposts, intending to halt there, reconnoitre, and attack the following day. Sher Singh, however, under cover of a long belt of jungle which lay in front of his position, moved out with all his force and cleverly manœuvred to bring on an action at once on ground of his own choosing, which afforded little opportunity for cavalry, and where with his superior numbers he could overlap the flanks of his enemy. After an hour's artillery duel a general advance of the British line was made in the after-noon. Lord Gough again took the bull by the horns, and, as was expressed on a previous occasion, found it "all horns." The dense patches of thorny bush which screened the Sikhs broke the ordered ad-vance of brigades, and the battle devolved into a series of detached combats—regiments singly forcing their way through the jungle to the open spaces, where they suddenly found themselves face to face with the enemy's guns and infantry massed by them. Then followed the volley, the cheer, the run upon the cannon's mouth, and fierce hand-to-hand fighting: gunners were bayonetted serving their guns to the last, and their infantry, in many cases after delivering their fire, dropped their firelocks and met the bayonet charge sword in hand, answering the "hurrah" with the Khalsa war-cry. One English regiment had sixty casualties from sword-cuts in capturing a battery, but the bayonet triumphed over the sword. The fight was waged with varying fortune in different parts of the field; each side could claim some success. From want of knowledge of the ground surprises awaited the British here and there. An impassable swamp, beyond which was posted a battery, effectually checked the advance of a brigade, which had to retire with heavy loss, but the other on its flank forged ahead and repaired the loss. The Sikhs fought gallantly and doggedly, as they did on the Sutlej. When their regular infantry retired they did so in good order, loading, halting, and turning to fire as if on parade: they belonged to the old well-trained Khalsa brigades, big, long-bearded men, clad in red coats. Darkness alone put an end to the deadly hurly-burly,

—to another soldiers' battle fought under the most adverse circumstances.

The Sikhs withdrew towards the Jhelum, retired within their prepared position masked by the jungle, and there fired a royal salute of victory, while the British bivouacked on the field of Chillianwala. Both sides sustained severe loss, that of the British being about 16 per cent of the force engaged, individual units suffering more severely than others, some dropping one-third and even one-half of their numbers. Heavy rain for the two following days prevented further operations, and on the third day the Sikh reinforcements joined. For a month the two armies lay facing one another, Sher Singh during that time making ineffectual attempts to induce his opponent to move out of his position, which covered the routes to the Chenab in rear. In the meantime Multan had fallen, and troops were marching up from there to reinforce the British. On hearing of their approach Sher Singh skilfully made a flank march by night along the front, and got a start of a day in an attempt to cross the Chenab farther up and make for Lahore; but on finding the fords guarded, took up a position round the town of Gujerat, where he concentrated 61,000 men and 60 guns, the finest and best commanded force the Sikhs ever assembled against us.

Lord Gough, having been reinforced, attacked the Sikh army early on the morning of the 21st February with 25,000 men and 96 guns, being for the first time in the two campaigns superior in artillery. The enemy's full power was now massed in front of him, prepared to fight a pitched battle. The blow that was to be struck would be all the more effective if dealt deliberately, without leaving anything to chance. For three hours all the British guns did deadly execution in the Sikh ranks, which they endured with stern resolution and tried their best to meet. In vain their infantry and cavalry attempted to advance to the attack; their bravery was of no avail against the murderous artillery-fire. Indian irregular horse charged and routed the Afghan cavalry. When the Sikh guns were nearly silenced a general advance of the British line swept the field, capturing 53 guns and all the camp with its *matériel.* The British casualties were 800, those of the Sikhs 7000.

The Sikh army had now been smashed on thoroughly scientific principles: no mistake was possible as to the decisive character of their defeat. Completely routed, they broke away in full flight to the north, pursued by the relentless cavalry, which inflicted further execution on them. A column of 12,000 men was promptly sent across the Jhelum to follow the wreck of the army and gather up all the fruits of victory. Sher Singh sent in to the British camp the English officers he had as prisoners, who had been taken when on duty with the Durbar troops. They had been well treated. He asked for terms, and received the reply, Unconditional surrender. The shattered Khalsa, flying north, were now nearing the Pathan country, where little mercy would be shown them by their hereditary foes. They were between the devil ahead and the deep sea rolling up behind them: annihilation was inevitable unless they accepted the British terms. On the 12th March 1849 they surrendered unconditionally. The Afghan contingent, after losing half their numbers, deserted their allies, and were hotly pursued by the British cavalry through Peshawar and driven into the Khaibar Pass.

At Rawal Pindi Raja Sher Singh, the Sikh commander-in-chief, with his sardars, one by one gave up their swords to the British general, and their men following grounded their arms at the victor's feet — most in gloomy silence, some in passionate tears on throwing down their cherished weapons, some reverently saluting them as they placed them on the ground, others muttering curses at their hard fate—all proud in bearing. They frankly acknowledged that they had been well and fairly beaten, and that now their cause was hopeless. They had been worthy and gallant foes, and were respected in their misfortune by their conquerors, who did not use their victory to humiliate them. The rank and file were furnished with means of returning to their homes. Back to their villages they went to toil, — to the plough again, — not as conquered enemies, but as free subjects of the Great Queen Victoria, to enjoy the same protection and privileges as the others under the British Crown. They would remain the same men as before; they had tasted of the salt of life, and its savour would never leave them. They had shed their blood in what they considered a good cause, and loyalty was still theirs to give, as we found so soon later on, when it was kindled anew after they recognised the spirit in which we met them and willingly grasped the hand held out to them.

With the crushing defeat of Gujerat perished the last hopes of resuscitating the Sikh kingdom. It was the final act of the tragedy which commenced on the banks of the Sutlej. The last stake had now been played and lost in a war exclusively of their own making. They had fought the British on more than equal terms; they were the first to draw the sword, and they were the first to lay it down and end the contest for supremacy by manly submission.

On the 1st February Lord Dalhousie, the Governor-General, always definite and specific in his ideas, declared that "the peace and vital interests of the British Empire now require that the power of the Sikh Government should not only be defeated but subverted, and their dynasty abolished." In his words, the victory gained at Gujerat was "memorable from the greatness of the occasion, and from the brilliant and decisive nature of the encounter,—it equalled the highest hopes entertained." On the 29th March 1849 he proclaimed that "the kingdom of the Punjab is at an end, and that the territories of Maharaja Ranjit Singh are now and henceforth a portion of the British Empire in India." All the inhabitants of the Punjab, sardars and people, were called upon to submit themselves peacefully to the authority of the British Government. "Over those who shall live as obedient and peaceful subjects the British Government will rule with mildness and beneficence, but if resistance to constituted authority shall again be attempted, if violence and turbulence are renewed, the Governor-General warns the people of the Punjab that the time for leniency will then have passed away, and that their offences will be punished with prompt and most vigorous severity."

The Sikh government went the way of all governments which will not learn to rule intelligently. The whole of the Punjab came under the British flag, which now waved over the continent of India from the sea to the Himalaya and Sulaiman Mountains. Little was it thought then of what the near future had in store for this land of soldiers. A few years later, when the storm of the great mutiny of the Bengal army suddenly burst as a bolt from the blue, the Sikhs were again in the field, but this time as loyal soldiers of their honoured Queen Victoria, fighting in her cause alongside their English comrades.

# CHAPTER XIII.

## THE 'GRANTH,' THE SIKH SACRED BOOK—RELIGIOUS OBSERVANCES.

The 'Granth' is the holy scripture of the Sikhs, containing spiritual and moral teaching. Its leading creed may be summed up in the words, The one God is a spirit, and is to be worshipped in spirit and in truth. It is written in verses, measured by quantity only, in the form of psalms, chants, and songs of praise. They rhyme together, intended for singing or intoned rhythmical recitation, great attention being paid to the rhyme. They are sung in public worship, especially in the Hur-mandar (the House of the Lord) at Amritsar, accompanied by stringed musical instruments. The book is written in the Punjabi dialect spoken by the people of the plains, with a mixture of Hindi idioms,—the character, a modified Hindi one, being called "Guru-mukhi" (out of the mouth of the Guru), used by the Sikhs in correspondence. All classes and castes are represented among the contributors besides the Gurus, — Hindu reformers, Brahmans, Jats, musicians, weavers, a Mahomedan saint, a holy woman, down to members even of lowly and despised castes, Nanak having preached, "God will not ask man of what caste or race he is; He will ask him what he has done."

The 'Adi-Granth,' the book of the humble Nanak, is held the most sacred, as the foundation of the Sikh religion. It was compiled by Arjun, the fifth Guru. After him a few verses only were added from the succeeding Gurus—a message from Tegh Bahadur, the martyr, while in prison at Delhi, to his son Govind, and the reply. The 'Granth of the Tenth King,' as it is called, that of Guru Govind Singh, concerns chiefly the ceremonial and social duties of his disciples—

THE GOLDEN TEMPLE IN THE SACRED TANK, AMRITSAR.

THE DURBAR-SAHIB, OR HEADQUARTERS OF THE SIKH CHURCH.

the Khalsa — and the practical course of their life.

The Sikh religion as it was founded by Nanak was a pure monotheism, the chief point in his doctrine being the unity of the Supreme Being. That the Supreme is One, and that there is none other, is over and over again inculcated by him.

> "Whom shall I call the second? there is none.
> In all is that one spotless One."

He alone, he said, is really existing, uncreated, endless, timeless, invisible, and indescribable — the Root of all things, the Source from which all have sprung.

> "He Himself is One, and He Himself is many."
> "From the Lord all the creation has sprung. By Himself the vessels are formed: He Himself also fills them."

Nanak's constant theme was personal love for a personal God, "More love to thee, O God." He strove to win his hearers to love and trust God, who claimed them as His creatures, to learn His sufficiency for all and everything. Scattered throughout the book are phrases like flashes of light, many of which parallel sentences in our own Scriptures, these thoughts and ideas being repeated in endless variations running into mystic darkness. Such phrases are: "Thou art my support, Thou art my trust, without Thee there is none other." "Wandering and wandering about, I have come and fallen in Thy asylum, O Lord." "Thou art my Lord, I am at Thy gate—O Lord, this is the prayer of Nanak, apply me to Thy worship." "Thou alone art the support of the helpless one, Thou art my strong protector." "What happiness shall I obtain without God? whose friend and beloved the Lord is, say, what may that man stand in need of?" "Our confidence is placed in God; He is my refuge — without Him I have not other assistance or reliance." "Thou art my friend and companion, my Lord, why should my soul be afraid." "True is the Lord, of a true name; in language His love is infinite. O Nanak, His worshippers are always happy." "Great is the Lord, of a great name, by whom creation is made. Higher than high is His name. His praise is continually in my mouth." "I sing the many and innumerable excellences of God; outside I sing, inside I sing, waking early I sing." "The Lord is merciful to the poor; Thou art my refuge. Thou art my hope." "Keep the eternal Lord in thy heart." "Who art on intimate terms with God, they remain fully satisfied with food."

> "Thou art the Creator, true my Lord,—
> What is pleasing to Thee, that will be done;
> What Thou givest, that I obtain;
> Without Thee there is none other."
> "Their faces are always bright in the true court of God."

There is much expressed regarding humility and the transitory nature of life, with its vanity, pride, egotism, idolatry, and malpractices:—

"Think not of caste: abase thyself and attain to salvation." "O brother, thy body and prosperity will not go with thee after death." "Man is but as the passing shade of the flying bird." "Wealth, youth, and a flower are guests for four days." "I may fasten a crown, royal hat and umbrella, on my head, I may be called a khan, king, or raja, but without God I am nothing."

"Who dwells in the house of the true one death shall not overcome. Who does crores [millions] of religious works but retains his selfishness, he incurs only fatigue. All his works are in vain." "The Lord is the strength of the weak. He neither comes nor goes. He is always firm." "At the last moment, O Nanak, none but God is any avail." "Fall at the feet of God; in senseless stone God is not; worship not another than God; bow not to the dead."

Although Nanak always spoke humbly of himself and confessed himself unlearned and the lowest of learners, the high position which the Guru occupied naturally led to his deification, and his disciples commenced to identify his successors with the Supreme Himself. It was therefore a fortunate event for the more free and moral development of the Sikh community that with the tenth Guru, Govind Singh, the Guruship was altogether abolished. Govind apparently discerned this. By developing a religious commonwealth he saved the Sikhs from sinking into a state of dull apathy to the world around them, to drifting into a community of monks, jogis, and fakirs. Nanak ever enjoined his disciples to remain in their secular occupations and not to leave the world, — that their religion was one of common life. He taught that the state of a householder was equally acceptable to God as retirement from the world; that salvation did not depend on outward circumstances, or in the performance of austerities, but on the inward state of the mind, which even in the daily business of life may remain absorbed in meditation on God. The evil practices of mendicant fakirs as well as the superstitions of the Brahman priesthood are frequently exposed in the 'Granth' and severely censured. His sound sense as well as that of Govind Singh saw that austerities, self-mortification, and penances in such a land soon degenerate a race. "No confidence whatever should be placed in jogis" (ascetics).

Nanak received all men as his disciples on an equality regardless of caste, for "in the other world there is no caste." Govind Singh finally abolished caste among his disciples, though the deeply-rooted prejudices of the higher castes refused to submit to this. He positively forbade the employment of Brahman priests in any capacity. He introduced a new ritual, partly taken from the 'Adi-Granth,' but mostly originating with himself. He appealed to the God of battles in his combat for a righteous cause, to defend his people against persecution, in his determination to form a nation, which he saw could not be effected unless they made the study of arms their aim and glory. Nanak the humble strove by personal example to inspire his disciples to live worthily, and after death to leave behind them the memory of a righteous life and good deeds, the only passports for the better life beyond.

In spite of all the abstruse definitions of the 'Granth,' the common people were contented to accept Nanak's definition of God, adapted for their everyday life and to meet inward and outward wants. The mystical speculations contained in the book as to the "higher form" and the *secret* were beyond their comprehension, but its teaching gradually "turned them from idols to serve the living God," and impressed them with the idea of one Supreme Lord, whom they could only realise as a personal, self-conscious Supreme Being, who creates all, governs all, and dispenses all according to His will.

Govind Singh did not make any change in the teaching of Nanak. He made the worship of the one Supreme obligatory and denounced idolatry. The additions he made in his 'Granth' are mainly regarding the duties of the Khalsa—the Commonwealth which he established. He received into it men of all castes and creeds on a footing of equality, and aimed at welding them into one religious and political body. To effect this he set up a number of ordinances binding on all.

In a Sikh household on the thirteenth day after a boy is born the father takes him to a Granthi (Scripture reader), who, after reading certain portions of the 'Granth,' solemnly lets it fall open wherever it chances. He then looks at the heading of the stanza where it opens, and its initial letter must be the initial of the boy's name, which is then selected from the stock of names which they have commencing with every letter of their alphabet. The *pahal* or Sikh oath of initiation may be administered to a boy when he reaches an intelligent age — at twelve or so — or at any age afterwards. There must be five Sikhs present to make this lawful. The candidate is dressed in a white tunic, and in the *kach* or tight white drawers reaching half way down to the knee, and is girt with a sword. The 1st chapter of the 'Adi-Granth' and Govind's 'Granth' are

BAPTISING SIKHS ON ADMISSION TO THE KHALSA BROTHERHOOD OF SINGHS.

read to him. He is then asked if he consents to be of the faith of Govind; on the reply, "I do consent," he is addressed, "The Guru is thy holy teacher and thou art his Sikh," and a solemn promise demanded from him to abide by the canons of the faith for the rest of his life. Then follows the ceremony already described in the chapter relating to Guru Govind Singh, of sprinkling a mixture of sugar-and-water, called *amrit* (water of life), on his head and face, and of drinking some of it out of the iron dish, exclaiming, "Wah, Guru ji ka Khalsa! Wah, Guru ji ka fatteh!"—Hail, Guru of the Khalsa! Hail, victory to the Guru! The warrior designation of "Singh" is then added to his name. He is now a Govindhi Sikh, and is commanded to wear always about him certain outward signs of the brotherhood, and directed how to keep and care for his *kes*, the long hair worn by Sikhs, how to knot it into the *jurah* knot on the top of the head, and which has to be taken down and combed out twice a-day. He is forbidden to cut or dye his hair or beard, to eat or drink uncovered, and to smoke or touch tobacco.

Every disciple is also enjoined to daily repeat some portion of the holy book. There are three prayers appointed for daily use: one in the morning before breaking fast, one before the evening meal, and one before going to rest. Idolatry, the worship of saints, and asceticism are prohibited. Hindu and Mahomedan ceremonies and religious books are not to be minded. He must never buy meat from a butcher, but eat only the flesh of such animals whose head was severed by a Sikh with a stroke of the sword. Beef is not so much as mentioned, as to eat it is considered an abominable crime, — sacrilege, — the cow being venerated as the favoured animal of the Almighty, whose preservation is a religious obligation, since it is so useful to man for domestic and agricultural purposes. The Govindhi Sikh adheres religiously to the command never to cut his hair. He will not even submit to this for a surgical operation, preferring to risk death. There is an old tomb extant outside Lahore, at a spot called "the place of martyrdom," in memory of a brave old chief, a companion of Govind's, who with 1000 Sikhs was captured by the Moghuls during the cruel persecutions in 1746. He was offered pardon on condition of having his long hair cut and renouncing his faith. He indignantly refused, saying, "The hair, the scalp, and the skull have a mutual connection. The head is linked with life, and I am prepared to yield it with pleasure." He and the 1000 Sikhs were all beheaded there and then.

Special attention is paid to the making and distributing of *karah prasad,* or consecrated bread, at their assemblies for administering baptism or other occasions, partaking of the character of a communion service. It is made of equal quantities of flour, butter, and sugar, mixed with water drawn from a well with an iron bucket and placed in a new jar. When prepared it is blessed and put on a stand round which the disciples sit praying, after which it is distributed by the Granthi, or Scripture reader, in equal portions to all present to eat. This is the love-feast of the brotherhood, when, according to Govind's injunction, "all must eat together and drink together from the same cup."

Every Sikh is enjoined to aid in the diffusion of the religion, and is not to have intercourse with the sectarians, of which several classes arose. They were accursed, and were to be treated as implacable foes of the faith. There are many other injunctions as to conduct and family matters, which Govind Singh insisted on as essential to rendering the Khalsa a select body, and to kindle their martial valour and hatred to the Mahomedans, whom he looked upon as the powerful persecutors of his race and the one bar against the attainment of religious freedom and national ambition.

One of the dogmas of the faith is equality of mankind, but this extends rather to religious tenets than to social laws. All Sikhs will eat consecrated bread and drink water one from another's hand except from the lowest classes, where caste is measured by occupation; but they will not intermarry. Each caste occupies a social position of its own, partaking more of family or race pride than of religious usage. It is maintained among the Jats mainly as a matrimonial system, social custom not permitting a man to seek a bride among the members of his own sub-clan. He must go afield to other septs of his tribe for a wife.

Among the Sikhs births and deaths should take place on the ground. The impress of their origin is still strongly maintained in their regard for the "Mother Earth," the ancient honoured deity. The strongest phrase to denote a human being is literally *earth.* "From one Mother is the world born." In the house, as soon as death approaches, the patient is taken off the bed and laid upon wheat-straw which has been spread on the ground. The dead body is carried to the funeral pyre on a wooden frame and placed on it with the head to the north, five Sikhs or more being present. The nearest relative takes a torch, and after walking three times round the pile of wood sets fire to it under the head. The earliest record of burning the dead is among the ancient Scythians, with whom the idea of purification by fire was universal.

Just as in the middle ages the strong nations of the West emerged from the bonds of religious superstition, so the Sikh reformatory movement took its rise at the same time, breaking away from the thraldom of the Brahman priesthood. It had its origin in small and peaceful beginnings on the part of humble preachers, — a low-class movement, conversion, not conquest, being its object. But cruel persecution gave it the impetus which culminated in secular power and kingship. The religion having

SIKH SOLDIERS (29TH PUNJAB INFANTRY) BURNING THEIR SLAIN COMRADES ON THE BATTLEFIELD AT PAIWAR KOTAL, AFGHANISTAN, 1878.

no venerable history like that of Hindu, Budhist, and Moslem, it has had much to contend with since the Khalsa lost its position as a ruling class fifty years ago; and for a time there was the danger under the powerful influence of Brahmanism, directed to overcome such a levelling simple faith, of it drifting into a backwater of Hinduism. But its robust strength has outlived this danger, and, according to the recent census of India, the Sikhs have increased considerably during the last decade. In a will case lately before the Punjab law courts, the decision was that the Sikhs at the present time are regarded only as a sect of Hindus; but the local Sikh organ, 'The Khalsa,'—its policy being to maintain the original reformed religion and worship of the Sikh Church,—protested that Sikhism differs widely from Hinduism in fundamental doctrine; that Sikhs do not consider themselves Hindus, and do not respect the Hindu pantheon or observe their religious rites; that Nanak, though born in a Hindu family, was not a Hindu, but established an independent religious sect of his own; and that "the day is not distant when thousands of Sikhs will be found disowning Hinduism completely, and priding in the name Sikh, just as converts to Islam and Christianity feel pride in calling themselves Muslims and Christians, and break off all connection with the creeds to which they previously belonged."

# CHAPTER XIV.

## THE SIKHS UNDER THE BRITISH CROWN.

The decisive element in ensuring future tranquillity and contentment in the Punjab after the annexation was the unequivocal nature of the British triumph, the liberal treatment of the vanquished, and the generous recognition of those sardars and others who had remained loyal to the treaty with the English protectorate. The great healing influence among the people was the knowledge that their lands were secured to them. The formidable Sikh army, which it had required so many hard-fought battles to subdue, was disbanded, and the turbulent soldiery settled down to industrial pursuits. They laid aside their national ambition and all schemes of hopeless political combination, and quietly accepted the new order of things; but their subjugation by no means signified their national annihilation. Religious liberty for all was proclaimed, and it was recognised to be a healthy and good thing for the Sikhs to maintain fidelity to the instincts and traditions of their religious convictions, which were not inconsistent with sincere allegiance to the British Crown; to maintain their sentiment of nationality in the form of subordinate patriotism; to keep in their recollection those elements which had contributed to the moral strength of the Sikh nation; and to preserve the character and enterprise engendered in their race by the trials they underwent in early times.

The Punjab recovered from the long-continued ravages of war with surprising rapidity. For good the old order changed, giving place to the new. Security for life and property following on disarmament soon reigned throughout the land. The growth of material prosperity among the people diverted their minds from the stormy past to assured hope of justice, peace, and plenty under a strong Government—to the protection afforded for the development of the many good qualities in them. Oppressive taxation was abolished, the land-tax reduced far below what it formerly was, and simple courts established in which the laws were administered with equal justice to all. Roads were made throughout the length and breadth of the province, and canals set agoing which made the waste places to blossom.

"Peace hath her victories no less renowned than war."

The ground-plan of the policy of Sir John Lawrence, the Chief Commissioner, was to maintain the status as he found it—to restore nothing that the Sikhs had taken. The chiefs were maintained in their states, and *jagirs* held were continued. By his character, firmness, and ability he soon won the confidence of all the people. He took them by the hand, he saw with their eyes, he thought with their hearts, and gave them improvements that they really wanted, not those which it might be considered they ought to want. This was the secret of his great personal influence, which secured for him a grip over the affection of the people that the events of 1857 did not loosen, but on the contrary strengthened. He proved the truth of an old Persian proverb, "To a just king his rayats [peasants] are an army," when a few years later he called forth an army from among them. He could not have commanded the Punjab and given it its place in the Empire had he not thoroughly understood the people and been in the closest sympathy with their characteristic traits, although at the same time he never allowed his sensibility to run away with his sense. It was this firm foundation on which the Punjab administration was built that enabled it to weather the storm which beat so fiercely on it in 1857.

A happy consequence of our wars with

the Sikhs was that we learned their great value as soldiers when mutual respect was won by valour in the field. After the first war some Sikh regiments were raised for our service, and after the annexation Sikhs were freely enlisted in the Frontier Force, and also in some regiments of the Bengal army, where they were not, however, welcomed by the Brahman fraternity, who resented intrusion on their own preserves as tending to break up their solidarity. One of the local Sikh battalions volunteered and was sent on active service to Burma during the war there in 1852, the vanguard of that movement for service over-sea to distant parts of the Empire which has characterised the Sikhs ever since.

In May 1857 occurred the great crisis of the revolt of the Bengal native army, which for a time threatened to overwhelm the British power in Upper India. Mischief was known to be brewing, but it was little suspected that the whole of that army was honeycombed with sedition and ready to throw off its allegiance. On the 12th of the month, "like a thunderbolt from a clear sky," a message was flashed along the wire to Lahore that the native troops at Meerut and Delhi had revolted, and that the ancient seat of Moghul empire was in the hands of the mutineers. At that time there were at scattered stations in the Punjab 10,500 English troops and 58,000 native; of the latter 36,000 were of the Bengal army, now known not to be trusted, the rest being Punjabi irregulars and military police, who not only stood true to their salt, but took a prominent part in suppressing the revolt.

Now was reaped the "rich blessing of Lawrence's vigorous and beneficent rule." The people under him were prosperous and contented; at the same time the outlook at first for the British was almost hopeless, but by prompt decision and action he saved the day, and his assured resolute manner restored confidence. The Punjab was not only quiet but actively loyal. The men who had so recently been our stoutest foes were now our staunchest friends, and in their splendid loyalty side by side with English soldiers beat down the Mutiny.

Within twenty-four hours after receipt of the startling news from Delhi the Bengal troops at Lahore, watching for the signal to rise, were disarmed; the forts there and at Govindgarh, Amritsar (the key of the Manjha, the Sikh home-land), secured, as also those at Ferozepore and Philor with the arsenals, while Sir John Lawrence personally wrote to the ruling chiefs that now was the time to prove their loyalty. Nobly they declared for the British Government.

The Sikh Raja of Kapurthala led 2000 of his men to take the place of mutinied troops, and afterwards marched them down to Oudh to fight by our side. The Cis-Sutlej states were nearer Delhi, and within the influence of the insurrection; but their Sikh chiefs did not hesitate to cast in their lot with the British Government, which had in old times thrown its mantle of protection over them and preserved their independence. The Raja of Jhind was the first in the field, declaring that he would abide by the British, under whom he had lived happily for fifty years. He cleared the road for the English troops advancing on Delhi. The Maharaja of Patiala supplied 5000 men, and held the line of communication between the Punjab and the British army before Delhi for a distance of 120 miles. The Raja of Nabha, with 800 of his men, occupied for us the fort of Ludhiana and escorted the siege-train to Delhi. The petty Sikh chiefs complained of it as a grievance if they were not called on for our service.

In the eyes of the Sikhs, Peshawar was the barometer of the strength of British power. It was the force of old habit in looking to the north, whence storms were wont to roll down on Lahore. "If Peshawar holds firm," said a wise old Sikh sardar, "all is well." He knew from experience what power it required to hold it firm in fair weather: if the British could do so in foul weather, all was safe. Lawrence's trusted lieutenants there, armed with the powerful factor of personal influence, aided the general in striking strong and quick blows at mutiny. Then the border Pathans at once appraised the situation and flocked to our standard. Three hundred Afridis of an outlawed clan were the first to come in, armed, begging to be forgiven and to be allowed to fight for us. They were incorporated in a new regiment being raised. Sikhs also about Lahore and elsewhere came in to be enlisted.

A movable column of picked men, English and Punjabi, was formed to patrol the country and dash down on the mutineers wherever they showed themselves. Terrible was the punishment inflicted on them. It was soon seen that the rebels at Delhi would receive no help from the Punjab. There was no more trouble from revolt in June. There were still, however, some 18,000 men to be watched, 6000 of them armed, among whom mutiny again showed its head in July, when they were nearly all destroyed or captured. By the end of July no more regiments remained to mutiny. Far below Delhi British power had almost disappeared: the few points held were like islets on the face of the dark waters of rebellion which had deluged the land. The rebel force at Delhi was now at its maximum—over 40,000 trained men holding that city, with 120 heavy guns on its walls, besides 60 field-guns, all of our own manufacture, manned by artillerymen from the revolted army.

The hundredth anniversary of Plassey saw a small British force, under 4000 strong, holding the ridge overlooking Delhi. It was increased to about 7000 early in July; but as yet, though constantly engaged with the rebels, no impression had been made on the city or a single gun silenced. Strenuous efforts had been made to reinforce it from the Punjab. The first to reach were the famous Guides of the Frontier Force, which marched 580 miles in twenty-two days, and signalised their arrival on the ridge by at once going into action: other corps of cavalry and infantry from the same force followed, pushing on with feverish alacrity to be in time, all animated with enthusiasm, which even infected the retired soldiers. It is related of an old Sikh officer, lately retired from the service, that hearing at his home of the Mutiny, and that his regiment was hurrying off to Delhi, he determined to rejoin it. The commandant found him waiting on the road with two swords by his side. He said he had come to command his former company, and had brought two swords—one to break over the heads of the rebels in the service of the English *Sarkar*, and the other on his own account. He was allowed to resume his old position, and was badly wounded early in the siege. Having recovered, he was present at the final assault. His company fell in that morning at the head of the column, much to his delight; but, owing to certain movements between the camp and the walls of the city, lost its place for a time. He rushed up to the commandant and loudly begged that the previous order of the companies should be restored, and that he should lead the attack. This was conceded, and the brave old warrior was killed an hour afterwards fighting among the foremost.

Nothing could surpass the heroic daring, the dogged tenacity, and invincible fortitude under privation and disease of the little army, with its exposed flanks and open rear, so gallantly holding the ridge during the trying hot season. There was no question of falling back,—Delhi was the vital point of the struggle for supremacy. It was to be taken at all cost.

Lawrence now sent on his movable column under Nicholson, his siege-train from Ferozepore, and the last English and Punjabi soldier that he could spare, keeping only a very small garrison in the Punjab, and then made his boldest venture by calling upon all the Sikh sardars to furnish soldiers of the old Khalsa army, adding, with a note of quiet resolution and self-reliance, "There must be no hesitation or delay on your part." By his vigour in beating down the enemy in the Punjab, in safeguarding it from the revolted sepoys, and in keeping the frontier inviolate, he had clearly demonstrated that the English were yet strong to punish or reward.

The time had now come for bold action in raising a new army to take the place of the old — to employ the fighting elements and banish dangerous temptation. The spirit of the Khalsa was roused by the scent of battle. They responded promptly to the summons and flocked to the British standard, many of them bearing the scars of the recent struggle. Those who were too old to serve sent their sons in their stead. The new army rose phœnix-like amid the ashes of military revolt.[1] Regiments of cavalry

[1] This army was clad in the now familiar "khaki"-coloured uniform which has been adopted by the British army.

and infantry were rapidly formed from the old Khalsa warriors and sent to the seat of war. A corps of Muzhabi Sikhs, 1200 strong, was raised from the workmen on the canals to serve as sappers before Delhi, and old Sikh artillerymen, who a few years before had fought against us, were sent down to work the guns in the trenches, where one of their officers astonished the captain of his battery by remarking that the rebels would not have made such fools of themselves if like him they had lived for a "month in Vere Street, Oxford Street"! He had been to London in the train of the Maharaja Duleep Singh, and had seen Britain's strength and resources, the object-lesson so epigrammatically expressed by Jung Bahadur, the great minister and ruler of Nepal, who had visited England, and who, when urged at that time to join in the effort to drive out the British, replied, "I have stood on London Bridge."

The army before Delhi having been reinforced by Nicholson's arrival, the assault was delivered with 5000 men on the 14th September, the anniversary of its capture by Lord Lake in 1803. After six days' severe fighting, endured with stern resolve, the British flag was on the 20th hoisted on the royal palace, and the whole city, which had been held by 40,000 of the enemy, was in our possession. The Sikhs at last, as triumphant victors with the English, stood on the spot where, 180 years before, their Guru, the father of Govind the Lion, met a martyr's death for refusing to abjure his faith. There was in existence among them a popular belief that they would, in conjunction with "hat wearers" (the British) who should come over the sea, conquer Delhi, and place the head of the Emperor's son on the very spot where the head of Guru Tegh Bahadur had been exposed by order of the Great Moghul. A Sikh officer who was present when the old King of Delhi was captured and his two sons shot, diligently remembering the legend, almost literally secured its fulfilment, and for three days the bodies of the king's sons lay on the spot foretold, close to the place where four months previously they had ordered and witnessed the massacre of forty-nine Christian captives, nearly all women and children.

The effect of the capture of Delhi was felt far and wide in the north, within and beyond the border. The Punjab had weathered the storm, and British prestige stood higher than ever. There was genuine rejoicing throughout the province, emphasised when the spoils of war from captured Delhi began to reach the villages. The pick of their men, old and young, came in crowds to join the new regiments, which were marched down as fast as they were raised to aid in restoring British power beyond Delhi. Upwards of 70,000 men were enlisted from the various races in the Punjab — Sikhs, Dogras, Pathans, and other Mahomedans, all differing in creed and customs, having little in common but a desire to fight for the English *Sarkar*, over one-third of this number being Sikhs, mostly trained warriors, the most valuable of them all. Never had the Punjab been so quiet. The border Pathans and the Sikhs had now, far from home, their fill of fighting, and freely they shed their blood for us.

While the battle was raging at Delhi the indomitable Havelock was fighting his way into Lucknow to relieve the beleaguered garrison there, a regiment of Sikhs forming part of his small devoted band. He effected this five days after Delhi fell. Sikhs from various mutinied Hindustani corps in Oudh had joined the little British force in the Residency and took their part in the famous defence. In far Bengal, Sikhs with our English troops were at the same time fighting against great odds, and the fine defence of a house at Arrah by some fifty of them with a few English civilians against vastly superior numbers of mutineers earned a special record for conspicuous gallantry. Even Sikh political exiles in Bengal aided our Government. Wherever the Sikhs were, they identified themselves with our cause and fought as lions of their race.

Towards the close of the year Lucknow, which had become the great stronghold and focus of rebellion, was finally relieved by a force under Lord Clyde, including in it troops sent down from Delhi after its fall. On that occasion, in the magnificent rush on the Secundra Bagh, a strong position held by the enemy in great force, the Khalsa war-cry was heard mingled with the Highland pibroch summoning to the onset, when stern Scots and Sikhs, intent on coming to close quarters with the foe, raced together to be the first in at the breach, a mere hole in the wall, than which, in the words of Sir Colin Campbell, who witnessed the assault, "there never was a bolder feat of arms." Until the close of the long campaign in 1859 the Sikhs were everywhere engaged alongside their British comrades in crushing out the rebellion.

As to the part the Punjab played in the great crisis of 1857, when the rebels

93RD HIGHLANDERS AND SIKHS STORMING THE SECUNDRA BAGH, LUCKNOW, 1857.

made a leap for empire, Lord Canning well expressed it when, after peace was restored, he addressed the chiefs at Lahore, saying, "In other parts of India I have received many distinguished chiefs of ancient lineage who have proved themselves faithful feudatories of the Crown, and many of lower degree who have been dutiful subjects in the midst of great discouragements and danger, but in the Punjab I find a whole nation of brave and loyal men." And the late Sir Charles Aitchison, a former Lieutenant-Governor of the Punjab, in his Life of Lord Lawrence wrote: "Certainly no troops ever fought more bravely or covered themselves with more glory than did the Punjab troops in our cause against the rebel sepoys. They shared with us the privations and diseases and dangers of the ridge, soldiers all day and sentinels all through the night. They shared in the glory of the assault. In the Oudh and Rohilkhund campaigns they were shoulder to shoulder with the best and bravest. They have sustained their reputation in many a hard-fought field since then. And what is more, there has sprung up in the Punjab a feeling of brotherhood to England and of loyalty to the Crown, which it will be our own fault if we alienate. In the spring of 1885, when war with Russia was imminent and preparations were begun for an expected campaign, many of the war-worn veterans of the Mutiny days came—with white hair and bent with the weight of years—to the present writer and laid their swords at his feet, recounting the favours and honours they had received, and begging, though too old and battered to go themselves, that their sons might not be forgotten when the roll for service was called." The subordinate patriotism of the Sikhs then came strongly to the front, and a wave of enthusiastic loyalty animated them at the prospect of war to oppose any attempt in India's direction.

The military revolt of 1857, one of

almost unequalled magnitude, was a gigantic effort to throw off our supremacy, which in the interests of civilisation it was our duty to maintain, and it needed the great struggle to bring home to all India the full significance of our mission there. The magnificent behaviour of the Punjab at that time, which so materially aided our cause, was a reflection of the generous treatment accorded to brave enemies and of their belief in our prestige, their loyalty being a matter of conviction and of genuine feeling.

When the Bengal army was reconstructed in 1860, the majority of the new regiments raised in the Punjab were incorporated in it. The Sikhs now started on a new extended career. In that year they formed part of the force sent to China, a field which ever since has had great attractions for them. Wherever during the last forty years the Indian army has served they have formed a valuable part of it. China, Abyssinia, Afghanistan, far Chitral, and Africa have been the scenes of their warlike exploits, where they proved that their martial ardour is as great as ever it was. They have penetrated to many parts of the vast African continent, East and West, where the British flag now flies, forming the backbone of local forces as legionaries of the Empire. Recently on the torrid plains of Somaliland a detachment of 200 of them fell to a man fighting against overwhelming numbers. To-day they are to the front amid the icy solitudes of high Thibet advancing our standard.

In almost every coast town in the Malay States and in China they are engaged as soldiers and police, being in great demand there as courageous and reliable men. For service they will go anywhere, being without fear of the unknown.

Though the Khalsa has ceased to be a political power, it has entwined its military, force with a strong chord of loyalty and sympathy for the British Crown. The profession of arms remains within the stream of their national life, and the title "Singh" is still with them what it was in their palmy days, one of military honour and glory and a badge of independence in religious thought. Their religion unquestionably encourages high moral and physical qualities. Whatever fighting they have set themselves to do for us they have done well. There is always an expectancy of great things from them, and they have done nothing to dispel this.

A tragic but glorious incident of the Tirah frontier campaign five years ago was the fall of the picket post of Saragurhi on the Samana ridge, with its noble garrison of twenty-one Sikhs, who belonged to a regiment lately raised and then in action for the first time. Attacked and cut off by an overwhelming force of well-armed Afridis, the little band fought for six hours, holding the walls, and with steady fire repulsing the enemy again and again with much slaughter. They were well supplied with ammunition, but it was only a matter of time with the thousands of the assailants to crush them out. Slowly but surely reduced in numbers by the Afridi marksmen, they fought on till the walls fell and only one Sikh was left. He defended the guard-room door, and alone shot down twenty of the enemy. Fighting with his face to the foe, the guard-room being set on fire behind him, he perished in the flames. The Pathans admitted having had about 200 killed and many more wounded. Nobly did these sons of the Khalsa uphold the traditions of the race in a locality where in bygone years the Singhs had so often fought the Pathans, and where hereditary animosities still hold remorseless sway. Well may the Khalsa be proud of their children, and Britannia also of such brave soldiers who know how to die in her cause. A cairn on the site of the post, a prominent obelisk close by, and memorials at Amritsar and Ferozepore, keep alive the memory of

SIKH CAVALRY AND INFANTRY OFFICERS AND SOLDIERS—INDIAN ARMY, 1903. (SERVICE DRESS.)

that signal proof of Sikh bravery and boundless devotion to duty.

They give far more proportionately to the Indian army than any other class of the population of India, and pass far more into the reserve after a few years' service with the colours. They are to be found in about eighty regiments, including those wholly Sikh and those in which they form a part. As military material they are admirable. Possessing a strong individuality, inured to hard labour and exposure from their early youth,—leading a healthy open-air life in their hamlets and villages, for they do not affect towns, — their home training is one to develop physical powers and to fit them for the hardest service in the field as soldiers. They combine a fine physique with energy, due to climate, occupation, and the northern strain in their character, the legacy of the old stock from which they sprang. Freedom from the trammels of superstitious caste ceremonies as inculcated by their spiritual guides, the stern and warlike nature of the iron creed of Guru Govind, the baptism of fire through which the nation passed in its early days, and the coherent rule of Ranjit Singh have undoubtedly stamped them with a national character, a marked trait in which is their reserved and self-respecting pride. Like Britons, the fighting spirit is built into them, and they do not lose it by years of peace. They still stand pre-eminent for military spirit and enterprise, proud of their order.

They are genial in disposition and independent in character, from their associates being their equals and from living on the products of their own lands,—more earnest and stubborn, after the manner of ploughmen, than impetuous,—better fitted for deeds requiring unflinching resistance, being gifted with a spirit which increases with adversity, and with bone to overcome difficulties. Frugality is very marked among them. A large part of the money spent on the army finds its way to the Punjabi villages, which, with what also comes from well-paid foreign service, are being steadily enriched, for the Sikh is too fond of his own country to settle abroad. All that can be saved goes to the homes. They do not waste money on the occasion of domestic ceremonies, as in other priest-ridden parts of India. As sons of the soil, the goal of their home ambition is land—more land and oxen to work it. Sikh wives are as free and independent as the men, and during the absence of the husbands remain at home in charge of affairs. On the annexation of the Punjab they were the first to appreciate the advantages of being subjects of the British Crown. When it became known that the English, who had conquered the Sikhs, were ruled by a Queen who was now their sovereign, they went in strongly for woman's rights and became a terror to tyrannical husbands. It is said that many a hard-fighting Sikh who had survived the battlefields found the scene of war shifted to his rebellious house, and again suffered grievous defeat.

During the last decade the Sikh population has become more numerous—by 13 per cent; and as the result of greater numbers of them being now enlisted, there has been an increase of those called Govindi Sikhs who have taken the *pahal.* They are held to make the best soldiers, the stern religious discipline enjoined by Govind engendering self-command, self-respect, and obligation to duty unto death through the talismanic influence of the Khalsa. When such as have not taken the *pahal* enlist, they generally do so at the hand of the Granthi or Scripture reader attached to every regiment in which Sikhs are in any numbers, and supported by them. They are the home missionaries of the *Durbar Sahib,* the headquarters church at Amritsar, who conduct religious services, read out the precepts of the 'Granth,' collect money for the income of the church, and keep alive the Sikh national and religious sentiment.

There was a remarkable demonstration of this sentiment at the great Durbar assemb-

MORNING PRAYERS AT THE SIKH CHAPEL IN THE REGIMENTAL LINES.

lage at Delhi in January 1903, when representatives of all races and castes were gathered together to hear King Edward VII. proclaimed Emperor of United India. At the suggestion of the venerable Raja of Nabha, a devout and devoted adherent of the Khalsa, the Sikhs decided to hold a memorial service to mark their peculiar sense of the deep significance of the Durbar by a solemn act of worship at the shrine of the martyr Guru Tegh Bahadur, who, they said, 228 years before foretold in the hour of his death the coming of the British Empire under which they enjoy religious freedom and personal prosperous liberty. It was a spontaneous act of loyalty managed all among themselves. As the birthday of Guru Govind Singh, the son of the martyr, occurred on the 6th January, it was decided to mark the day signally. The story of the martyr's death and prophecy was retold, , and how this was the time and place to repledge their loyalty to the British, who under the guidance of God fulfilled the prophecy.[1]

A small temple in the chief street of Delhi marks the site of Tegh Bahadur's execution in 1675. A procession in all the panoply and pageantry of old feudal Sikh days proceeded to this spot. It was formed of horsemen, banner-bearers, and the Sikh levies accompanying their chiefs, being followed by a carriage in which under a covering of gold was the sacred 'Granth,' the holy book. This was reverently lifted out and conveyed into the shrine, whilst to mark the special importance of the occasion the English national anthem, "God save the King!" was played by the musicians. All the Sikh chiefs, sardars, and church dignitaries were there. It was

[1] According to Sikh tradition, Tegh Bahadur surrendered himself into the hands of the Moghul Emperor with full knowledge that he was about to lay down his life for his people. But Aurungzebe hesitated to kill him, and sought by promises and threats to induce him to embrace Islam. At last, all such proving fruitless, he was brought before the Emperor on the charge of having raised his eyes from the prison walls to the

a gathering of the nation, called together by their own leaders, and all knew what they were there for. Standing by the holy book, they, on behalf of all the Sikhs, with their martyred Guru present in spirit (they all believed that), renewed in each other's presence their vows of fealty to the King-Emperor. A sacred chant was then sung in which all joined, closing with their invocation to the Supreme Being, which was responded to by the loud shouts of the crowd. On the sacred 'Granth' being replaced in the carriage, "God save the King!" was again played, to emphasise the meaning of the ceremony which typified their loyal and sacred bond to British rule

latticed windows of the palace zenana. He knew that this meant death, but he fearlessly answered, "If I have raised my eyes in the direction of thy zenana, it was not to look upon its forbidden windows but far beyond them into the mist, whence I saw armies of a fair-haired race pouring forth from beyond the seas who shall tear down thy purdahs and overthrow thine empire." This prophecy, according to the Sikhs, was fulfilled to the letter in 1857, when the small British force—5000 to 40,000 of their foes—shook down the treacherous throne of the Moghuls, an avenging act in which they also played a part.

and the compelling force of the union which, according to their ideas, had been miraculously brought about.

This striking incident is a significant proof of Sikh veneration and affection for the British Crown, the effect of which has doubtless been widespread. It marked their sense of identity of interest in being a co-ordinate unit in the majestic whole of the Empire, treading the same path under the guidance of Providence. It followed the important ceremonial of the Durbar, the outward form of the great idea which so profoundly impressed them and touched their imaginations.

The aged Raja of Nabha, who initiated the memorial service, was unable from the state of his health to come to the King-Emperor's coronation in London as a representative of the Punjab. He was a notable figure in the Sikh procession. Simply clad in white from head to foot, his long snowy beard adding to the dignity of his features, he alighted from his carriage

HIS HIGHNESS RAJA SIR HEERA SINGH OF NABHA, G.C.S.I., G.C.I.E.,
COLONEL OF 14TH FEROZEPORE SIKHS, INDIAN ARMY, 1903.
(A NOTABLE SIKH CHIEF.)

some distance off from the shrine and walked on barefooted, with slow and solemn steps, through the crowd, who bowed reverently as he passed. A few days before, at the great Durbar held to hear the proclamation announcing the Coronation of his Majesty the King-Emperor of India, when all the chiefs tendered their felicitations and assurances of homage to the Crown, he added to his the few eloquent words, "Now I can die in peace, as I have discharged the three duties of a true Sikh—I have lived according to the precepts of the Gurus, I have aided the State with my sword, and now I have paid personal homage to my sovereign."[1]

The Sikhs are no longer illiterate as they were in the old days, when they despised the pen and looked on the sword as the one power in the land. Now they see that the pen is sometimes the more powerful of

[1] Contingents from the armies of the Sikh states have ever, from the days when they came under our protection, aided their suzerain in war.

the two, and at least that education does not weaken the hand that wields the sword. Though nominally a minority—a powerful one—among the mass of the population in the Punjab, which in fact is more Mahomedan than Hindu, they are socially and politically of the highest importance, as they constituted the dominant class at the time of the annexation, and still form the great majority of the gentry in the regions of the five rivers. Their military aristocracy supply the Indian army with excellent officers. They gather thickly in the districts round Amritsar, the Mánjha, or middle home of the Sikh nation, the nursery of their most revered Gurus, their most powerful sardars, and Ranjit Singh's most redoubtable warriors. There a third of their numbers are now found, the rest being scattered in the Sutlej states and throughout the province; large colonies of them having also recently settled along the new canals taken off from the rivers, running south through the extensive plains where the Jat tribes from time immemorial roamed with their flocks and herds—plains of dormant fertility, which now with the magic touch of water produce splendid crops of golden grain. Railways have been made through the irrigated lands, and there numerous villages and towns have risen from which on a gala day, when a Viceroy or a Lieutenant-Governor visits them, thousands of old soldiers come forth wearing their be-medalled uniforms,—men whose sons follow their fathers as soldiers of the King-Emperor. These settlements form extended lines of defence, where the many owners of the small farmsteads may be depended on to fight for their own should the day ever come of invasion again from the north. They have no fear of invaders, whoever they may be. It remains true for all time that on a hardy spirited peasantry an empire's strength is stayed.

Though the Punjab is not blessed by nature like the rich tropical Gangetic valley, it is fruitful in bold and enterprising men.

This is the secret of its great prosperity at the present day. Nowhere in India are the peasantry more flourishing and contented, as it was Lord Lawrence's policy fifty years ago to make them—to become the bulwark of the Indian Empire in the north. His Royal Highness the late and lamented Prince Albert Victor of Wales, on his visit to Lahore in 1890, when replying to the address presented to him there, felicitously referred to the Punjab as "the soldiers' land," adding, "There is no province in India that can boast, as the Punjab can, that it is the bulwark of defence against foreign aggression, or that can be termed with the same significance the guard-room of the Eastern Empire."

PRINTED BY WILLIAM BLACKWOOD AND SONS.